CONQUERING
THE
PAPER
PILE-UP

About the Author

Organization and time management expert Stephanie Culp is the author of several books, including *How To Conquer Clutter* and *How To Get Organized When You Don't Have The Time*. She is the motivating force behind the concept and principles of the company that she founded in the Los Angeles area, The Organization. The Organization designs and implements systems and establishes procedures to help businesses and people get, and stay, organized.

As a national lecturer and seminar leader, she has addressed countless groups, including the National Accounting and Finance Council, the Specialty Equipment Market Association, members of management at MCA Universal Studios, and the Tupperware National Jubilee Convention, where she addressed 14,000 people.

Stephanie has been featured on hundreds of radio and television programs across the country and is regularly interviewed by newspapers and magazines as well. Her articles have appeared in such publications as the *Los Angeles Times*, *Redbook*, *Family Circle*, and *Working Woman* magazines.

In 1986, Stephanie was elected as a delegate from Southern California to the White House Conference on Small Business in Washington, D.C. She has received an award for Outstanding Contribution to the Profession of Organizing from the National Association of Professional Organizers, of which she is also a founding member and past president. In addition, Stephanie belongs to the Author's Guild and the National Speakers Association. She lives in Los Angeles.

STEPHANIE CULP

CONQUERING
THE
PAPER PILE-UP

Writer's
Digest
Books

Cincinnati, Ohio

For the University of Southern California, and the gifted doctors there whose care and talents changed my life:

*Dr. Dennis-Duke Yamashita, D.D.S.
and Dr. Richard J. Van Gemert, D.D.S.*

Conquering the Paper Pile-up. Copyright © 1990 by Stephanie Culp. Printed and bound in the United States of America. All rights reserved. No part of this book may be reproduced in any form or by any electronic or mechanical means including information storage and retrieval systems without permission in writing from the publisher, except by a reviewer, who may quote brief passages in a review. Published by Writer's Digest Books, an imprint of F&W Publications, Inc., 1507 Dana Ave., Cincinnati, Ohio 45207. First edition.

Library of Congress Cataloging-in-Publication Data

Culp, Stephanie.
   Conquering the paper pile-up / Stephanie Culp.
      p.   cm.
   Includes index.
   ISBN 0-89879-410-2 (pbk.)
   1. Paperwork (Office practice) — Management. I. Title.
HF5547.15.C85   1990
651.5 — dc20   90-12676
                                                                                           CIP

Design by Clare Finney

CONTENTS

Introduction

Acknowledgments

I've written several books now, and with every book, I seem to be surrounded and helped by the same core group of great people. First and foremost there's the publisher, Writer's Digest Books, a company that treats me with the utmost integrity. There I work successfully with Mert Ransdell, Jo Hoff, John Andraud, and Hugh Gildea. They all contribute enormously to the writing and publishing process in countless ways, not the least of which is that they put up with me with heroic grace and patience.

Freelance editor Beth Franks gives all of my work the sensibility, shape, and polish that is needed to turn a manuscript into a book and that only a talented and trusted editor like Beth can provide. Lorrie Briscoe of JBL Graphics and Pat Hickey contributed most of the graphics, with Shu Yamamoto's work rounding out the visuals.

And on the home front, Jim Reed and Fritz Culp continue unstintingly to provide affection, amusement, and accolades that keep me motivated.

Whenever I slip and start to think *I* wrote and produced a book, I stop to review the names of those who contributed so much and pause to thank everybody. *We* did it! Thanks!

INTRODUCTION

Have you ever wondered about the modern-day phenomenon known as the "paperless" society? If today's society is so paperless, what are those stacks of newspapers, magazines, important documents, bills, and miscellaneous papers doing all over the place? And what about the infernal mail, which arrives mercilessly by the virtual truckload every day? If you are drowning in the daily deluge of paper, or if you've got a paper problem that is backed up in boxes, bags, and piles, this book is for you. If the paper in your office is out of control, this book is for you. If you want to reorganize and streamline the household accounts and family records, this book is for you. Or if you want to set up a home-based business or reorganize the files of the small business you already own, this book is for you. Even if you don't really have a paper problem but want to set up a workspace to accommodate papers that you know will soon be flooding in, this book is for you.

If you're suffering from a paper processing system that doesn't work or if you don't even *have* a system, this book will give you the plan you need to either refine your current system or set up a new one altogether. You'll learn the basic principles of moving the mail as soon as you get it, and you'll read about creative ways to organize and store different types of paperwork. With this information, you can clean up your act at home and in your office. In business, once the paper principles in this book are put into effect it's easy to analyze the overall paper flow and spot any potential paper saboteurs or even incompetent employees who have been covering up. At home, you'll discover a tremendous sense of relief as you finally introduce some order to those important family and financial records.

Whatever your paper problem, rest assured you are not alone. Millions of people are awash in paper and are looking for a simple solution to this time-consuming fact of life. This book provides simple solutions to paper management and storage and promises to make it easier to keep a piece of paper, to lay your hands on a piece of paper when you need it, and to do it all with a minimum of stress in the shortest amount of time possible.

The bottom line is that whether it's your personal paperwork or your corporate paperwork, this book will help you regain control over the papers in your life; as a result, you'll become more productive and reduce some of the stress that piles of paper invariably cause in anyone's life. That's a promise.

Much success!

CONQUERING
THE
PAPER
PILE-UP

PART ONE

MOVING PAPER MOUNTAINS

PAPER-NOIA: A MODERN AFFLICTION

They say we are living in the Information Age, and indeed, there does seem to be a staggering amount of information to be gleaned from every imaginable source. Books, magazines, newspapers, radio, and TV all bombard us with information daily. Letters, memos, faxes, reports, photocopies, bulletins, bills, and trade journals add to the glut. Computers have made access to information (and *mis*information) instantly available with just the flick of a few buttons. And although computers and other electronic information processors were supposed to herald the beginning of the paperless society, with a steady and slightly obnoxious clackety-clacking sound, computer printers all across the country are kicking out enough paper to wallpaper the world.

This abundance of information has given rise to the phrase "information anxiety." This, roughly translated, describes what a person begins to feel when he or she feels obligated to soak up as much information as possible on a daily basis, and when this becomes overwhelming, those feelings of obligation turn into anxiety. The information freak starts to suspect that there simply isn't enough time in the day to keep up with these self-inflicted, unrealistic expectations. Contributing to and even worsening the anxiety is the vehicle that delivers the information — paper.

As the paper arrives, the information-anxious folks adjust their level of anxiety upward several notches with every few inches of papers that get added to the existing piles of papers with information yet to be absorbed. The overworked and understaffed small business watches the papers multiply at a frenzied rate, and the owner starts looking for the panic button. The pack rat just keeps mindlessly and religiously collecting, until one day the health or fire department is called in. The socialite dives headlong into charitable activities, and when the papers start to accumulate and then — horrors! — require her attention and action, she announces that her trip around the world starts next Monday. Someone *else* will have to tend to this paper problem.

Know the Early Warning Signs

I could cite dozens of examples of people and paper from my experience as a professional organizer, but the fact is that, whatever the circumstances, paper is something that nearly everyone would probably rather do without. And having to deal with piles of the stuff just exacerbates an already bad or, at the very least, inept attitude. Taken to the extreme, all of this paper-phernalia can result in what I like to term paper-noia, which is a debilitating set of attitudes that can result in bizarre concepts such as the idea that paper should be piled, not filed and the feeling that every piece of paper that comes into one's life needs to be hoarded for an indefinite period of time.

These attitudes are not always surprising. The constant barrage of paper can make it difficult to find the time to figure out how to manage the problem, let alone actually *do* something with all that paper. If you haven't taken care of yesterday's or last week's mail, there is no way you are going to have time to take care of the paper that gets dumped on you today. Then, if you're not careful, paper clutter sneaks up on you. Before you can say "booby hatch," papers are popping out of drawers, boxes, and bags. Piles can be seen collapsing on top of tables, desks, filing cabinets, and refrigerators. In a futile attempt to maintain control over the ever-growing problem, you stuff the papers into baskets, trays, and file folders, some to be lost forever. Since the daily deluge of paper somehow seems necessary to life as we know it, culling the junk papers from the important papers can be a formidable task. Even more challenging is figuring out how to keep a piece of paper so that when you need it you can actually find it. Without some sort of paper management system, utilities can get turned off, credit card accounts canceled, and friends and relatives can turn on you in response to their unacknowledged letters and invitations. You get to go to court because you lost your driver's license or car registration and received a ticket while driving without that all-important piece of paper. If a spouse dies suddenly, and the survivor can't lay his or her hands on documents such as the marriage certificate, simple things like the burial arrangements can be stalled, adding more anguish to an already painful situation. Lost phone numbers can result in late appointments, and misplaced notes and bills in unhappy clients or botched deals. Finally, things slowly grind to a halt, and your secretary starts thinking about checking out the rates at the funny farm — and maybe she's checking on rates for herself, not just for you. Because people with paper-noia drive everyone around them crazy as they consistently forget, lose, and otherwise hopelessly mismanage their mail and daily paperwork.

And while people with paper-noia are driving others crazy, the paper is driving *them* crazy. Desperate, they finally look for some kind of professional help — and not the psychotherapeutic kind either. Desperation usually gives birth to a strong desire to get something done about the papers, *now!* They know, deep down, that if they could get their papers in order, they'd be more organized, more productive, and under less stress. And they're right. Not only that, they'll have more time for themselves and will find that their image gets a healthy boost almost immediately. (A clean desk is *not* a sign of an empty mind — it's a sign that an efficient, productive person works there!) Over the years, I've worked with and trained count-less people and businesses who wanted their paper picture transformed. Regardless of what the paper problem may be, I know it can be organized to provide relief and clarity and to impact the bottom line (whatever your bottom line may be) positively. Let me give you just a few examples:

The therapist. Although the therapist's patient files were in good order, he had a lifetime's worth of other papers in rather astounding quantities. His biggest problem was that he had fallen into a three-by-five trap, and by the time I got to him, he was floundering like a dying fish. The three-by-five trap can best be described as an addiction to index cards. This guy was really hooked. On the cards, he wrote insights, addresses, lists, things to do (one thing per card, of course), birthdays, quotations, and ideas for his next book, as well as other notes written in shorthand that no one but he could read. He also had an index card system for the books in his library and another for his writings. The real capper was the index card system where he would note, again, sometimes in shorthand, in which drawer certain papers could be located. He needed that because all of the papers were so out of order and, in many cases, duplicated that he couldn't find what he needed most of the time. This one index might have worked, except that those particular cards were mixed up with all of the other cards (are you still with me?), some of which went back as far as 1947. And, of course, he had a follow-up index card system that made sense in theory but that in reality was mind-boggling. He had *thousands* of cards. His life was somehow intertwined with those cards, and finally everything of a productive nature, particularly where any kind of paperwork was con-cerned, slowly ground to a halt for him. The first step in getting him orga-nized was to get him off his card habit. Like withdrawal from any addiction, the process was painful for him, but in the end he did see the wisdom of it. I left him with an organized filing system that included only *one* index card system to record anniversaries and birthdays. Demanding total withdrawal from his index card habit seemed cruel and unfair, and he was content with the results of a system that still allowed him *some* index cards.

The health care company that was held hostage. This health care company called me when their entire filing system became undecipherable. What they didn't tell me at first, but what I discovered as I worked on the project, was that they had been in what I like to call a "hostage" situation. The employee in charge of the files had deliberately set up and then worked with a system that nobody but she could understand. This method of opera-tion is also known as insuring your job security. She had so much seniority (along with a friend in a high place) that she probably had all the job security she needed without sabotaging the files. But she trashed them anyway—just to be sure. The result was that nobody could find anything without turning to her for help. You couldn't even file anything *into* the system, even if you wanted to. It was such a mess that figuring out what drawer to open was impossible. Eventually something hit the fan, and I was called in. The employee responsible for the mess was not happy to see us, but she cooperated because she had no choice. Refusing to cooperate was useless because we went through every single piece of paper in the bank of filing cabinets—with her or without her, it was going to get straightened out. Before we left, there was a five-minute training session with the principals of the firm. I call it Filing 101. Five minutes is all it takes because the system we install is so simple. Even executives can grasp it. I did have the distinct feeling that since the executives were standing there for this training session, some definite changes were going to be made regarding who was responsible for what pieces of paper in the company. Paper sabotage can backfire on you if you're not careful.

A death in the family. One day I received the news that a young man I knew had died suddenly. His widow was beside herself trying to cope with the shock of his death, the burial arrangements, and the like. The young man was a collector, and it took two days of working virtually around the clock just to locate pertinent documents such as their marriage certificate and his military records, both necessary for making burial arrangements and other financial transfers. Insurance records were buried in mountains of other paperwork, as were the title to the car and other ownership records. It was some time after his death before we were able to cull out and organize the important documents of his life. It was an anguish that I hated to see his widow experience—having us, virtual strangers after all, going through her husband's things immediately upon his death. We tried to be compassionate, and she tried to be patient. This was not the first estate-related paper problem I'd worked with, but no matter how much experience one has, it is wrenching to see the survivors in such pain. It is never easy for anybody to have to deal immediately with paperwork before they've even started grieving.

Paper pack rat. Paper pack rats don't usually care about changing their ways, but one day, some years back, we got a call from a paper pack rat who claimed to want to tackle her problem in her house. When we arrived, we discovered newspapers stacked in the living room, some dated as far back as 1966. Needless to say, the living room was impassable. The family room was stacked waist-high with more newspapers and with bags and bags of coupons. The bedrooms were full of papers in boxes along with other clutter. You could get to the bed in each room if you had to, but that was about it. Pack rats are extraordinarily resistant, and this pack rat was no exception. Nevertheless, we managed to completely clear the living room and one bedroom. We made good though incomplete progress in her bedroom, and then we started eyeing the family room. Here, our pack rat dug in her heels. Those bags of coupons were her DMZ. She started going through the coupons one by one — and there were *thousands!* The newspapers in that room as well as a good portion of the ones that had been shifted from the living room were also logjammed in the family room. These she was simply bundling up with string and moving back. She had purchased a freestanding shed, and she was moving newspapers and coupons, one stack at a time, into the shed out back. We were, in effect, moving the mess around and accomplishing almost nothing. I did what all of her relatives had done long ago, and what any sane person would do under the circumstances; I gave up. A person can only do so much with a certified pack rat.

Home librarian. Then there was the woman who had a seat on the New York Stock Exchange. She was also a great patron of the arts, and she had four-drawer filing cabinets full of papers. She had methodically installed a filing system based on information that she had gleaned from a book on the subject of filing. The problem was that it didn't work. Based on an index and numbering system (rather like a library), it took a few exasperating extra minutes' search to locate any file in the system. We had to dismantle the system altogether and set up one that made some simple sense.

Those are only some of the paper problems I've personally solved. Every time I go into a small- or medium-sized business, the paper crisis screams for attention in nearly every area, from the files to the mail room. Because it's not enough to store it effectively (although that certainly helps); you need to *move* the paper effectively once it comes in the door. I've trained people who operate one-man shops how to deal with the mail in a timely manner, and I've analyzed how employees, as well as the presidents of larger companies move papers from point A to point Z. I've cleaned up the backlog (mess), worked out simple paper flow systems, and written it all down in manuals. I've trained thousands of salespeople to organize their paperwork and surroundings. In short, I've taught individuals and businesses how to make effective paper flow methods and storage work for them to make their lives easier and more successful.

I've taken all of this experience along with some of the tips from my other two books, *How To Get Organized When You Don't Have the Time* and *How To Conquer Clutter,* and put it to work for you in this book. You'll get paper tips in a number of areas, from how to organize your desk to how to set up a simple filing system and how to decide which papers to file and which ones to store or toss. Today nobody can escape the paper avalanche, so I've covered paper problems in the home as well as the office. On any given day, mothers, children, executives, secretaries — nearly everybody, when you think about it — get blessed with more papers than they ever dreamed possible.

HOW TO USE THIS BOOK

To get the most out of this book, you'll need to begin by finding out just what your paper problems are. You can do this by completing the Paper-noia Profile on pages 8 and 9. The rest of Part One will help you *get started,* whether your problem is in your home or in your office. This section will help you decide what to do with each piece of paper. You'll discover how to make those keep/toss decisions by using a simple paper processing system. You'll also find out how to organize your desk and workspace and how to set up a filing system that will work for you, regardless of your paper circumstances.

Once you've tackled the basic principles of paper organization, turn to Part Two, Paper from A to Z. Here you'll find solutions to a variety of specific paper storage problems for that all-important gotta-keep paper-work. This easy-to-use alphabetical listing lets you turn immediately to the information that will help you with your particular paper problems. If you only have a few trouble spots, you can quickly find your alphabetical answers without reading the entire book. If you're starting from scratch or need to completely overhaul your current system, you'll want to use Part Two as your reference guide when you set up your files.

Finally, Part Three, Keeping Paper In Its Place, provides some guidelines for purchasing equipment and supplies and a quick review of the basic principles of paper management, organization, and storage. In this section, you'll find new tips on maintaining your files every day, week, month, and year. And you'll find out how ten minutes each day can make a difference all year long in your paper-prone life.

Now that you're in the mood to do something about all that paper, use the following checklist to find out how severely you are affected by that awesome modern affliction known as paper-noia.

PAPER-NOIA PROFILE

Here's your chance to check your personal paper-noia profile to find out if your paper problems are getting out of hand. Simply put a check mark by the items that describe your situation; leave a blank by those that don't apply to you.

☐ Do you have so many "to do" lists that you don't know where to begin, and you spend part of each day reorganizing these lists?

☐ Do you have scraps of paper scattered all over the place with bits and pieces of information noted on them?

☐ Have you reached the point where you find yourself deliberately not opening the mail for days at a time? (After all, you haven't taken care of yesterday's mail; how on earth can you face today's?)

☐ Does the top of your desk look like the national archives? Is it so cluttered with piles of paper that you don't have any space left to do your work?

☐ Do you tell everyone around you not to touch a thing on your desk because, in spite of the apparent mess, you know *exactly* where everything is?

☐ Do you have some kind of legal or accounting problem pending that could have been avoided (be honest!) if you had been more organized? (You didn't pay a parking ticket; your taxes are overdue; someone is taking you to small claims court.)

☐ Has your telephone, electricity, or other utility been turned off, or have your credit cards been stopped, simply because you forgot to pay the bill (because you misplaced it) and not because you didn't have the money?

☐ Do you always wait until the last possible minute to try to gather and organize your records for tax purposes?

☐ Do you keep old newspapers and magazines you haven't read because there's something very important that you *must* read in each paper or magazine? Are the stacks growing daily with no real relief in sight?

☐ Do you have piles of papers in your house or office — stacked in boxes and piles or stuffed in bags — all waiting for the day when you have the time to go through them all? (You keep telling yourself, If only . . . if only I had the time . . . if only I had two more filing cabinets . . . if only I had a bigger office. Do you have the "if only's"?)

☐ Does it seem like you and your staff are struggling daily with the apparently unending propagation of piles of paper?

☐ Do you often have a hard time deciding what to do with the paper in your life (figuring out where to *put* it is particularly difficult for you)?

☐ Are there papers in your hold basket that have become permanently pending for no particular reason?

☐ Are there papers in the files that are older than you are?

☐ Are you completely out of space and desperately in need of more room for paper storage?

☐ Do you or your staff spend some time nearly every day looking for misfiled or lost papers and documents?

☐ Do you often find that a piece of paper that you filed yesterday is not there today, and you don't have any idea where it is?

☐ Have you come to the realization that you have no idea what happens to a document or piece of paper when you are finished with it?

☐ Do you spend what seems like a fortune on office supplies, but still find that when you need something (a new file folder, a notepad, a pen that writes) you can't seem to lay your hands on it?

☐ Does everyone blame everyone else for the paper problem, yet no one has the time or the solution to effectively eliminate the problem?

☐ Have you been putting off organizing your paperwork because you think you are the only one who can do it, and you don't have the time to do it right now?

☐ Have your colleagues, friends, or relatives started making snide comments about your paper clutter?

Scoring

This profile was designed so you wouldn't have to spend a lot of time figuring the mathematics of scoring. Simply give yourself one point for each check mark.

1-4 Congratulations. You have only a small paper problem that you can probably easily correct yourself. More than likely, you're just a bit behind, or it's time to bite the bullet and do some purging to get back on the productive paper track. Tips in this book will help you do just that.

5-8 Uh, oh. You've got a paper problem that, if not corrected now, will turn into a crisis before you know it. Use this book to clean up the backlog and streamline how you handle your incoming load of paper.

9-12 If you feel you have totally lost control, chances are you have, or are about to. You can regain control of the paper in your life by using this book as a guide to cleaning up your paper act. You'll need to commit a good chunk of time to the project, however, or you'll just find yourself dangerously threatened by an avalanche from your paper mountain.

13-22 Good grief. It looks like you are definitely drowning in the daily deluge of paper. If you think you are suffering from paper-noia, you have good reason. Paper chaos is probably a way of life for you. It's time for an organizational overhaul, no question about it. Use this book (and, if necessary, hire someone) to help you implement a good system for all of your papers, old and new.

OVERCOMING INFORMATION OVERLOAD

As I've said, the plethora of paper in our society all too often leads to "information anxiety," which in turn is a prelude to total information overload. I see this condition all the time in my clients, whose inner need to *know* and *have information* has become compulsive, obsessive, and addictive. If your paper problem has reached the information overload stage, you'll need some extra help when you sit down to deal with your backlog of papers. You're a candidate for extra help if you've got magazines, newspapers, and catalogues that go back several months, if you're sitting on several weeks' worth of unopened mail, or if you can't see the tops of your desk, counters, tables, or any other surface because of the piles of papers. If the stacks are propagating in boxes, bags, and piles in closets, storerooms, and around the rooms in your house or office (propped up against any available wall space), you are definitely into overload. Way into it. In this case, you may have to call a professional organizer. But before you do that, try doing it on your own. First, schedule a block of time to devote exclusively to this paper organizing project. Then make yourself stick to the following rules:

Do one thing at a time. Clean one drawer or go through one stack of papers until you finish it. Don't spend a few minutes organizing one area followed by a few minutes organizing another area.

No phone calls. Don't take any, and don't make any.

Don't allow distractions. No visitors, TV, or stopping to read an article in a magazine you pick up.

No eating! Stop to eat only if it is breakfast, lunch, or dinnertime. If you are at home, stay out of the kitchen, and at the office resist the urge to take a trip to the vending machine or cafeteria for a coffee break.

Confront your fear of letting go. Hoarding paper is mentally exhausting and can get in the way of your success. Give up your need to control through information hoarding by letting some of it go.

THE BOTTOM LINE FOR BUSINESSES

As you pause to consider your paper problem, wondering where the paper comes from, where it should go, where it went in the past, and finally, how you can lay your hands on it again, consider the following:

Contents of the Average Four-drawer Filing Cabinet

- One drawer in four often contains active records that are needed on a regular basis;
- One drawer in four will often contain inactive records that could easily be sent to low-cost storage or tossed altogether;
- Two of the four drawers will often be empty or contain supplies or other noninformative materials (such as food, shoes, or purses).

Taming the Paper Tiger

- The typical office generates twice as much paper as it needs to by mindlessly photocopying dozens of copies of a single document;
- Eighty percent of everything that is filed is *never looked at again;*
- From one third to one half of everything that is currently filed could probably be either tossed or moved to low-cost storage;
- Once something goes to low-cost storage in an off-site storage facility, it probably has a less than 15 percent chance of ever being looked at again.

The High Cost of Storing Paper

- A good four-drawer filing cabinet is expensive — with prices that generally range from two hundred to three hundred dollars;
- Prices for lateral-style filing cabinets are slightly higher than for vertical cabinets, and fireproof cabinets can cost four to five times as much;
- Legal-sized file cabinets in either lateral or vertical style are at least 15 percent more expensive than letter-sized cabinets, and the supplies that go in them can be as much as 30 percent more expensive;
- With allowance for an opened drawer and standing room, the typical vertical style, letter-sized filing cabinet requires approximately seven to eight square feet of floor space, with legal-sized filing cabinets requiring about 25 percent more space than the letter-sized cabinets. At an office space rental rate of ten dollars per square foot, a vertical letter-sized filing cabinet will occupy seventy to eighty dollars' worth of floor space per year;
- Don't forget the cost of labor for sorting and filing the papers into the cabinets. Assuming you have a file clerk who files at a salary rate of ten dollars per hour and spends only three hours each week sorting and filing, the cost of those services over a year's time would be $1,560.

Whether you are paying hundreds or thousands of dollars in equipment, supplies, and services to sort and store your papers, the cost of storing paper is soaring. No wonder everyone is spending so much time trying to catch the tiger by the tail!

The paper principles in this book will help you catch and tame that paper tiger, so you can handle your office paperwork as efficiently as possible.

Setting Up a Paper Processing System

To tackle a serious paper backlog (you've got papers stacked all over the place, and the filing cabinets are full to bursting), the first thing you need to do is gather up all of the loose papers and files. Get all of the papers from the top of your desk, as well as papers stacked or piled on top of the filing cabinet, bookcase, and floor. If you are dealing with a paper problem in your home, make sure you check each room and gather up all the papers that are stashed on top of bureaus, in closets, and on top of the refrigerator and kitchen counter. Put all of the papers into one huge stack. If your stack is so tall that it will topple, get a large carton or two and put the papers in them.

Once you've assembled all of the loose papers and files in one area, it's time to sit down and methodically go through the papers, *one piece at a time.* Begin by remembering this simple paper-processing principle:

There are only four basic things you can do with a piece of paper.
Understand that, and sort your papers into these four categories:
To do

To pay

To read

To file

Throw the rest away. (To get yourself in the proper frame of mind for this, put a large garbage bag at your side.)

It is important not to get sidetracked with worry at this point. You are only *sorting* now, so don't start worrying about how you should respond to the latest correspondence from your attorney, or why the credit card company didn't give you that credit that was supposed to go through. *Just sort.*

To Do. Once the entire pile (or piles) has been sorted, go through each category again. Begin with the papers in the To Do pile, and ask yourself these questions:

Do I really need to do this? If not, get rid of it by filing it or dumping it.

Is it too late to do this? If it really is too late, get rid of it by filing it or dumping it.

Do I really want to do this? If the answer is no, find somebody else to do it, even if it costs you money. After all, you've probably got more important and/or fun things you could be doing.

Does anybody care if I do this? If the answer is *no,* then you shouldn't care, either. File it or dump it.

The papers that are left in your To Do pile after you've gone through it should be only the papers that you really have to do something about.

To Pay. Next, go through your To Pay pile again. Ask yourself these questions:

Has this already been paid? If it has, mark it paid, and file it.

Is there a problem with this bill that I need to look into? If the answer is yes, you might want to move it into your To Do pile so that you can make the call or do the research necessary to straighten the problem out before you actually *pay* the bill.

The bills that are left in your To Pay bin after you've gone through it should be only the bills that you really do have *to pay*. I'd tell you not to worry about these bills, but that's silly. Bills are made to worry about. Just don't let it stop you from continuing your sorting project.

To Read. Next, go through your To Read pile. Whatever you do, *do not* allow yourself to stop and read the magazines, journals, or catalogues in the bin. Instead, quickly scan the material's table of contents or cover and ask yourself these questions:

Is there a sound reason that I must read this? If the answer is no, *dump it.*

Do I have time to read this? If the answer is no, *dump it.*

Is this out of date? If you've got reading material with outdated information in it (such as old catalogues and sales materials and journals that have been replaced with new editions), *dump it.*

Do I have more than three months' worth of issues here? If you have magazines backed up for three months, bite the bullet and get rid of at least one month's worth. You're never going to catch up with your reading as it is.

Once you've dumped as many magazines, newspapers, and journals as you can, review the remaining reading materials and, with a pair of scissors and stapler, cut out any articles that you need to read and staple them. Toss the rest of the magazine, journal, or newspaper away and put the article into the bin. Tomorrow, over breakfast or during a break, you can finally read that article that you've been meaning to get to.

To File. Finally, go through your To File pile. When you did your initial sort, you thought you had to keep those papers. After all, that's why you tossed them into this pile. Now it's time to think again. Remember that 80 percent of everything you file you will never look at again. Remember how expensive it is to allocate space to paper storage, and finally, remember how much time it takes to actually *file* those papers (because that's what you'll have to do sooner or later—they can't stay in the bin forever).

With those thoughts firmly fixed in your mind as you go through this pile, make a commitment to decide what to do with each piece of paper, once and for all. We'll cover files in more detail later, but you really have three filing choices with these papers. You can: 1) file them in the Archival files; 2) file them in the Current files; or 3) file them in the Circular files.

Archival files are generally kept in a transfile box (available at office supply stores) and stored in a closet, warehouse, garage, or off-site storage unit. Papers that should be kept and stored include financial and legal papers that you are required by law to keep for a specific period of time, but that you are not using on a regular basis. There are no concrete rules about the length of time these documents should be kept, and entire books have been written about these records' retention requirements. To evaluate which of your important records need to be kept and for how long, check with your certified public accountant, your attorney, or the IRS. Once you've decided to store records, make sure that the storage area is clean, dry, and free of bugs and other vermin, otherwise all of your records will eventually get ruined.

Current files include papers that you might use as a resource on a regular basis, and current financial, legal, and business or client files. Preferably these files will be kept in a filing cabinet, but you may want to break them down a bit more by priority. For instance, you could put papers and files that pertain to a current project you're actively working on in your desk or in a convenient file cart (for more on this, see Types of Files, pages 33-37, and Organizing Your Desk, pages 18-26).

Circular file. Finally, there are the papers that you put in the To File bin that really belong in the Circular file. This file is also known as the Trash. The beauty of it is that you don't have to spend the time or the money to set up a file before you put the papers into the trash can or garbage bag. All you have to do is *dump it.*

DECIDING TO DUMP

If you have trouble letting go of paper or can't decide what to dump, ask yourself the following questions as you pick up each piece of paper to help decide whether or not you should *dump it:*

Is it a duplicate? If it is a copy of something you already have, *dump it!* Keeping copies "just in case" is unnecessary. And forget about sending some of the copies to your friends, relatives, and colleagues. They've got enough paper in their lives; they don't need more from you.

What's the date? If it is hopelessly out of date, *dump it!* This includes catalogues from two seasons back, invitations for events long since passed, and price and address lists that have changed.

How much will it cost me to store it? Remind yourself constantly of the cost of paper storage, and if you'd rather spend your money elsewhere (like on a trip to Europe), *dump it!*

Is the information on this piece of paper relevant to my current lifestyle? If it goes back to when you were a hippie, and now you are a yuppie, *dump it!*

How often will I need to refer to the information on this piece of paper? If you don't know the answer to that question but want to keep the piece of paper "in case you need it someday," *dump it!* That's an excuse, not a reason.

Do I need this piece of paper or do I want it? There is a big difference between *need* and *want,* and if you want it but don't need it, chances are very good you should *dump it!*

Do I really have time to read this? Be honest. Do you really have time to read all those trade journals and pieces of junk mail? If you're too busy to turn around now, chances are you'll never get that stuff read. *Dump it!*

Will I really use this information? Will you really try out this new recipe, or are you just clipping it out of habit so you can stuff it in the drawer with all of the other lip-smacking untried recipes? Will you ever take a trip to Tahiti, or are you just filing it in a fantasy file? If you know you won't use the information, *dump it!*

Is quantity more important than quality? If you've got reams of paper that pertain to one area of your business or personal life, do you really need that quantity? Or could you pull out a selection of the best and go for quality? This goes for your college papers from ten years ago, children's school papers, personal correspondence, and sales and promotional materials from your business's early years.

Does someone else have this information? If you really did need to lay your hands on this information ten years from now, could you get it from another source, such as the library? If the answer is yes, *dump it!* Why waste space and money storing something you only need once in every ten years. Let the library do that for you.

And finally, you can take what I call the *Earthquake Test:*

Could I live without this piece of paper? This question is also known as the "what's the worst thing that could happen" test. If a major earthquake occurred tomorrow (Californians take note), or if you were wiped out by fire or flood, would you need this piece of paper? (If you can't answer this question with an immediate yes or no, turn to the Disaster Recovery Plan on pages 46-49 to find out what really matters in a disaster.) If, on the other hand, you know in your heart that you could live without that piece of paper, do the right thing and do it now. *Dump it!*

A System for All Seasons

To create a permanent paper processing system, simply set up baskets for the four basic categories: To Do, To Pay, To Read, and To File.

Make your To Do and To Pay baskets out of two stacking wire baskets. Do not get fancy, fussy, colored plastic baskets. Go to the stationery store and get the old-fashioned wire kind. They still work best. You can see into them so you always know how much work is there, and there's plenty of room for your hand to reach in and grab the papers. Fancy smoke-colored boxes, that, when stacked, are impossible to work with quickly become paper traps. When they fill up, the tendency is to just add other baskets on top and to keep dumping more papers into them, ignoring the piles below. Get rid of these if you have them and switch to the wire ones (which are much more difficult to stack at will, removing that temptation altogether).

Make your To Read basket out of a roomy basket with a handle on it. Cart the thing from room to room (if you work at home) if you like, but keep it off the top of your desk. When the basket gets full, tell yourself that you have to toss something out before you accept one more thing in your life to read!

Make your To File basket out of a large wicker basket (a pet bed works well) or an oversized wire basket (such as the kind used in rolling carts). Now put it *under* your desk and toss those papers to be filed in there. This eliminates at least 60 percent of your desktop clutter and repetitious paper shuffling on top of your desk.

Finally, don't forget the trash basket — you'll be dumping a lot of paper from now on. But come to think of it, instead of throwing it all away, you should really start **recycling** paper. Most cities have several recycling companies; some have even instituted municipal collection programs. Look in the Yellow Pages under "Recycling" and call to see what they'll accept. Most will recycle everything except "coated news," the kind of paper magazines are printed on, and papers with foil or plastic adhered to them. The financial remuneration ranges from about two to six cents a pound, but

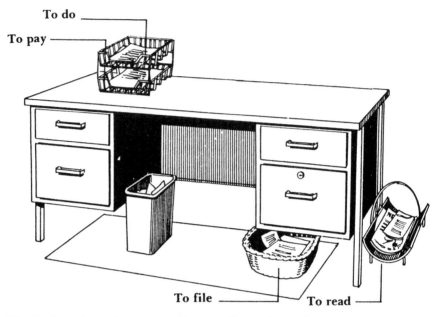

Use the four-step system to prevent paper pile-ups by sorting your papers as they come in. You'll also make life a lot easier if you keep a two-drawer filing cabinet next to your desk. That way you can pull files and refile them without getting out of your chair.

Shu Yamamoto

unless you own a printing company, you aren't into recycling for the money. People recycle paper because it conserves one of the world's most valuable resources — our trees.

ORGANIZING YOUR DESK

Desks have somehow become the paper dumping ground for millions of Americans. If you have a desk at home, your spouse dumps papers (like the bills, for instance) on your desk that you swear have nothing to do with you. The kids dump school papers and art projects. The mail, books, magazines, newspapers, and coupons all land mysteriously on this, your sacrosanct surface. What's so aggravating about all this dumping is that none of those papers has anything to do with the papers that are *supposed* to be on your desk — you know, the ones *you* dump on the desk.

If you work in an office, it's more of the same. The mail is dumped twice a day by a shipping clerk who is happy as a clam (because he or she is *getting rid of papers!*). Your boss drops by and throws some papers in your face, demanding that you generate even more paper in response. When you go out to lunch, you come back to pink phone messages all over your desk (and sometimes taped to the chair). Trade journals and memos are mixed in with notes, phone numbers, reports, still-to-figure-out expense reports, invoices, and yesterday's mail.

And, oh, I know; it's not your fault. You don't have enough time to do everything. And, don't touch anything, cuz you know exactly where everything is. And, there's a method to your madness. And, oh yes, an empty desk is the sign of an empty mind, don'tcha know.

Well, I've heard all of those excuses and more. And so have the other people around you (this includes your spouse, your boss, and your customers). And I'd be willing to lay money down to bet you that this is what your messy desk says to them:

- This person is disorganized (and therefore not too competent).

- This person doesn't manage time well (and therefore can't be trusted with important documents that have deadlines).

- This person obviously has trouble making decisions, since he or she can't decide what to do with all these papers (and consequently I'd better not entrust this person with anything that requires in-depth decisions).

- This person is trying to look busy and important with all this clutter (and I don't need to deal with somebody who tries to bluff me out with piles of papers).

- This person is overworked (and if he or she can't handle current responsibilities, he or she will never be able to handle my job or a promotion).

- This person lacks discipline and is untidy (and I certainly don't want him or her making a mess of my things).

For those of you who have a small but very messy desk at home, here's some of the things that little desk says about you:

- Chances are pretty good that some of the bills don't get paid on time around here.

- This person obviously is not in complete control of the household.

- There are bound to be at least a few "lost" pieces of paper buried in one of the piles on this desk.

- Behind a messy desk is someone who can't keep house properly.

- This person probably doesn't manage his or her time or the family's time well.

So the next time someone walks over to your cluttered desk and makes a comment or "joke" about the mess, you might want to listen up. Because regardless of whatever excuses you might offer, your desk says a great deal about you that you aren't saying about yourself. If you want to clean up your personal and professional image, a good place to start is by cleaning up your desk. You'll find that you have less stress and are more productive with an efficiently organized desk. Your organized desk will now say that you are professional, competent, efficient, organized, productive, and in control.

Step 1: The Desk Purge

To begin organizing your desk, first empty the drawers and remove everything from the top of the desk. The following items are usually found in and on the average desk:

Equipment

Office Supplies

Personal Items

Reference Booklets and Manuals

Files

Loose Papers

As you remove everything, group like items together. Stack all the loose papers in one pile, and group all the office supplies together, with all the stationery organized, and all of the paper clips together, for example. Throw away things that are obviously trash as you go.

Equipment. First, check the lighting on your desk and make sure it is adequate. If it isn't, now is the time to get more lighting or upgrade the bulb. Next, replace the equipment on the desk, making sure that it is positioned for maximum ease and efficiency. If you are right-handed, put key equipment such as the adding machine and typewriter to your right. If you have too much equipment to put back on your desk, consider putting the phone, for instance, behind you on a credenza or table so that you can turn your back to the door when you take calls, thus discouraging passersby from dropping in. Or, if you have equipment that you use regularly but not every day, such as dictating equipment, this could go behind you as well.

If your desk is a small one at home, make sure that any equipment you use regularly, such as the phone and Rolodex or address book, is placed conveniently on the desk so that it is easy to reach and use on a daily basis.

Most equipment should be placed to your right (unless you are left-handed), moving clockwise around the work area. Here is an example of efficient equipment placement:

Calculator	Extreme right side of desk, within easy reach at all times.
Clock	Right side of desk, above the calculator.
Lamp	Front right corner of desk above clock.
Typewriter	On typewriter extension that pulls out on the right side of the desk.
Lamp (swing arm type)	Clamped onto typewriter extension for extra light over machine as needed.
Telephone	On top of a two-drawer filing cabinet, next to the typing extension.
Answering Machine	Next to phone on top of two-drawer file cabinet (the Rolodex is here as well).
Electric Pencil Sharpener	On credenza behind desk.
Dictaphone	On credenza behind desk (not used that often).

With this equipment placement plan, all of the key equipment is within easy reach with just a quarter-turn of the chair. With a half turn of the chair the dictaphone and the pencil sharpener—both of which are used only occasionally—are instantly accessible.

Office Supplies. Your desk should have some drawer space for storing office supplies. Keep a selection of regularly used supplies in your desk and store extra stationery and supplies elsewhere (either in a supply cabinet, on a shelf, in a closet, or if you are working at home, don't forget under the bed). If space is at a premium, limit your office supply orders. You don't need a gross of any one thing; you just need as much as you can comfortably store. Some supplies are generally kept on top of the desk, with the rest of the selection stored in a drawer (or cabinet).

DESK TOP OFFICE SUPPLY CHECKLIST

You may want to keep these items on top of your desk or credenza so that they are always immediately at hand:

- ☐ Calendar
- ☐ Letter Opener
- ☐ Note Paper or Phone Message Pad
- ☐ Paper Clips (in container)
- ☐ Pencil Sharpener
- ☐ Pens, Pencils (in container)
- ☐ Rolodex (next to phone)
- ☐ Stapler
- ☐ Tape Dispenser
- ☐ Post-it Notes

Other office supplies that need to be in or near your desk can be stored in a variety of ways. Small supplies can be organized with drawer organizers. Stationery can be efficiently stored in a desk drawer with a divider insert tray. Forms that you use every day can be stored on a metal stationery storage rack that you can put on your credenza within reach (again, do not buy plastic racks). Or you can use hot-file racks, mounted on the wall above your desk or on the side of a filing cabinet next to your desk to hold forms and stationery supplies; another option is to store forms and paper supplies in hanging file folders in your desk.

BASIC OFFICE SUPPLY CHECKLIST

Keeping a selection of basic supplies at hand, with excess or back-up stored in the office supply cabinet (elsewhere), can streamline your operations at your desk. You will probably want to keep these working supplies in or very near your desk:

- ☐ Express Mail Supplies (if you use Express Mail frequently)

- ☐ Forms (that you use frequently)
- ☐ Invoices
- ☐ Note Paper, Legal Pads, or Steno Pads, (depending on your preference)
- ☐ Paper Clips
- ☐ Paper Punch
- ☐ Pens and Pencils (be sure to throw out pens that don't work)
- ☐ Postage
- ☐ Post-it Notes
- ☐ Rubber Bands
- ☐ Checkbook
- ☐ Ruler
- ☐ Return Address Labels (a great time-saver when paying bills)
- ☐ Scissors
- ☐ Stamp and Stamp Pad
- ☐ Staple Remover
- ☐ Stationery and Envelopes
- ☐ Tape

As you put the office supplies back into your desk, make sure you toss out old, irrelevant stationery, business cards, and rubber stamps. Also get rid of old, useless forms and pens that don't write. Here you'll need the most important office supply of all, the *wastebasket*. Get a big one; you're going to need it before this is over.

Personal Items. Personal items include everything from tea bags to shoes to photos and awards. Put the awards on the wall or on a bookcase or shelf. Put a small selection of photos on the bookshelf or on your credenza, and, if you must, one photo on your desk. Remember that this is a *work* space, where personal touches are nice, but should definitely be kept to a minimum. Nobody needs to see your entire family tree in photographs, from Great-aunt Minnie down to Puff the pooch. If you're short of space, check these family photos out first. They may just be crowding you out. Any food should be kept in the kitchen or cafeteria. If this isn't possible, consider investing in a very small picnic basket or cooler that you can tuck under, or next to, your desk to hold your lunch rather than letting it occupy precious desk drawer space. Walking shoes, too, are more aptly stored discreetly under the desk rather than in a drawer. A plant is fine so long as it is in good shape and doesn't create a cluttered look on your desk.

Reference Booklets and Manuals. If these are used regularly, they can be stored on a shelf mounted above the desk or in a wall-mounted hot file. If they are used only occasionally, they can be stored on the bookcase or in the credenza. Some booklets can be filed (such as the instructions for the phone answering machine—once you've mastered its operation, of course). Toss all out-of-date materials without hesitation.

Files. Generally these go in the filing cabinet. If you are actively working on the files, you can store them temporarily in your desk file drawer, where you can also keep other "working" files; or you can store them in a rolling-basket system that you can adapt as your "project storage unit." If you opt for this kind of storage, remember that once you are done with the file, or if for some reason the working file is no longer needed or relevant on a regular basis, it should be moved to the permanent file storage area (usually a cabinet). If you want to keep files near you, but there are so many that the desk drawer or cart won't hold them all, then go with the two-drawer filing cabinet that you can place next to your desk so that it becomes an extension of your desk. (You can use your desk file drawer for forms and stationery in this case.) For more on what to do with files, see pages 32-45, "Setting Up Your Files."

Loose Papers. All of the loose papers that were in and on your desk need to be gathered up into a stack or two. Then go through the papers, one piece at a time, and sort them for *action*. Once you have dispensed with these papers, *never store paperwork inside your desk again*. Out of sight is out of mind, and eventually you will overlook or forget to process some crucial piece of paper because it is buried in a drawer.

Step 2: Using the Paper Processing System

Now that you have worked your way through the desk purge, set up your equipment, and laid in an efficient stash of office supplies, you are ready to start dealing with the *paper* that comes into your life across the desk. You can begin with the stack of loose papers that you have gathered up from on top of and inside your desk. These papers should be quickly sorted into the four baskets that are the cornerstone of the Four-Step Paper Processing System (as discussed on pages 12 and 13). Make sure your To Do and To Pay baskets are within easy reach on top of your desk, with the To File basket under the desk and the To Read basket either to the side or behind the desk.

In/Out Baskets. Once you've sorted and organized all of the loose papers, there is still the matter of the papers and mail that come in and go out on a regular basis. No doubt this is why the In and Out box system was dreamed up and adapted. In and Out boxes represent the prelude and the finale to the Four-Step Paper Processing System. All of the new mail and paperwork that arrive during the day go in the In box. Once you have processed everything, invariably there are papers and pieces of mail that need to go Out—either to be mailed or distributed to other people. These go in the Out box. This time-honored In/Out system is still a workable concept, since you can see at a glance what you have yet to go through (and to sort, and then, you hope, to do); for papers that are going Out, it provides a way to get them off your desk, into a box, and ultimately out the door.

In and Out boxes should be clearly labeled and should be either wood or wire since these boxes are the roomiest. To keep things simple, yet distinct, I recommend that you put your In and Out boxes someplace other than your desktop. If you have a credenza behind your desk, you have the perfect spot for the In box. If necessary, however, another option is to have the In basket on the left front corner of your desk and the To Do and To Pay baskets behind you on the credenza.

If you have no support staff, try placing things that are going Out on a "to go" table. Pick a spot near the door and either allocate part of a bookcase shelf (if it is next to the door) or set up a small table to hold things going Out. This can include the outgoing mail, dry cleaning tickets (and, for that matter, the cleaning), and your handbag or briefcase and keys. You might have to take a step or two to put things on the table throughout the day, but it will help keep your desktop clear and will mean that you won't forget anything as you walk out the door.

Desk Working Files. If you have a number of "working" files that you use every day, or if you are involved in a project that means you need to access several of the same files every day, you may want to set up a desk filing system. You can do this by putting the files into hanging file folders in your desk file drawer, or you can set up a portable hanging file rack right

This hot-file organizer can be mounted on the wall next to or over your desk or on the side of a filing cabinet or other metal cabinet. Use it for files you need access to throughout the day.

JBL Graphics, Montrose, California

on your desktop (these racks are available at the stationery store). You can also store often-used files in wall-mounted hot file racks, but this only works if you have a small number of files—once the rack is holding more than three or so files, it becomes difficult to see what's in it. You can also set up a portable rolling cart, which I recommend for project files, since this cart usually holds more than the average desk file drawer.

And you can use these desk file drawers, racks, and carts to hold stationery supplies and forms (this is particularly useful, for example, for a real estate agent who needs to have a large quantity of forms available for easy access).

Remember, though, that "working" files imply just that—your are always working with them. When you don't need to work with them any more, they should be stored in the regular filing cabinet. Outdated forms should also either be moved or tossed. If you have more files than can be accommodated in a cart or drawer but need them close to you, a two-drawer filing cabinet next to your desk will give you immediate access to the files at all times, since the cabinet will essentially be an extension of your desk.

STREAMLINING YOUR OFFICE

Where you put your papers, whether they are stored or easily accessible near or in your desk, can make or break you in terms of organization. If, for example, you have to get up from your desk and walk into another room to the filing cabinet, chances are you won't do it. Instead you'll start a little stack of papers just "for now." For now turns into forever, and the next thing you know, you've got papers everywhere, with the active ones happily comingling with the papers that should have been filed a long time ago.

So, think about where you will position your desk (work area) and where you will position your filing cabinet(s) (storage area). You'll want your desk to be in a pleasant location, where you feel comfortable working. If you don't like to face a wall, put the desk so that you look out a window. If you sometimes work from home and have no room for a desk, you can turn the dining room or kitchen table into a desk, with rolling carts kept nearby to hold supplies and active records. You can even set up a portable work area next to your bed by using rolling carts and a bed table like those used in hospitals. Remember, though, that if you have a significant amount of paperwork to process on a daily basis, you will probably have to forego bedside or kitchen table approaches in favor of a traditional desk that will give you space for daily work and active storage for supplies and records.

Bear in mind traffic patterns and don't set your work area up near a lot of activity. You'll be interrupted constantly, and chances are good that others will use your work area as a dumping ground for their own things. If you work in an office, often the position of your desk can invite interruptions that you don't need. If you are facing the door, passersby see that as an invitation to drop in, and if you have a comfortable visitor's chair, once they've collapsed into the seat, they're like a horse, impossible to get up and back out of your office. To reduce these time-wasters' visits, try positioning your desk so that you do not face the door, and eliminate the visitor's chair or put it across the room so that the visitor has to physically pull it up to your desk. (Most people won't be this forward, and if you have someone important coming in, you can always pull the chair up yourself.)

Choosing Functional Furniture

As you establish an organized paper processing center (this is also often known as your office), consider the furniture and equipment you should buy in order to make paper pushing as painless as possible.

But before you shop for furniture, you'll need to carefully consider the volume of paper you process and/or need at hand. Don't go out and buy a beautiful antique French desk with one dinky drawer in it if you get and process fifty pieces of mail every day. In fact, don't get one of these even if all you process is fifteen pieces of mail each day. They are not functional and serve only decorative purposes. Paper pushing is serious business, so do some serious shopping.

FUNCTIONAL FURNITURE CHECKLIST

Assuming you are serious about organizing your papers and have the space, I generally recommend that you have at least the following functional furniture:

☐ *Filing Cabinet* — You'll need at least one two-drawer filing cabinet. *Warning:* Make sure you get a *full suspension* filing cabinet. This ensures that the drawers glide smoothly and that you can easily see and reach all of the files in the drawer. Many inexpensive cabinets do not have this feature, making it difficult to store and retrieve papers on a daily basis. You'll also want to make sure the drawers are fitted to hold hanging file folders (if they aren't, you can purchase portable racks to insert from your local office supply store). A good filing cabinet will last just about forever, so buy accordingly. Place this cabinet near your desk for fingertip access to files used on a regular basis.

☐ *Desk* — Your desk should (preferably) have at least one drawer that holds files and one drawer that will accommodate small office supplies.

☐ *Cabinet or Bookcase* — A cabinet or bookcase, small or large, wood or metal, is perfect for keeping binders, manuals, reference books, and office supplies.

☐ *Equipment Platform* — If you have equipment, it needs its own workspace next to your desk (a typing extension or stand for the typewriter or a computer stand for computer equipment).

☐ *Project Storage Unit* — This will provide you with a holding/sorting area for projects in progress (this can be a credenza, a table, or a rolling cart).

☐ *Chair* — Get a comfortable chair on wheels. Make sure it does a good job of supporting your back.

☐ *Lighting* — Make sure you have adequate lighting for the desk and equipment platform areas. You will want to have enough light to illuminate the entire room when necessary, and you can also benefit enormously from additional lighting over specific areas (such as your computer station or the area where the typewriter is placed). Table lamps, extension lamps that clamp onto the desk, and track lights are all possible lighting sources that can be used to provide adequate lighting for your work area and room.

The Layout

Measure your space, taking careful notes on where doors, windows, and critical outlets are located. Take those measurements with you when you shop, along with a tape measure. By making a rough layout on paper before you purchase your furniture, you can check measurements against your available space and avoid ordering anything that won't fit.

Don't be afraid to be creative. If you are setting up a home office in a spare bedroom, you can put a lateral filing cabinet at the end of a bed as a "footboard," with a television or radio on top for guests. Or you can use a filing cabinet with three or four drawers to divide a space in a room. A two-drawer filing cabinet can be placed next to your desk to put files at your fingertips and give you extra horizontal surface area that can hold your calculator or phone and phone answering machine. A bookcase, regardless of the number of shelves, can be used for functional as well as personal purposes. You can store binders and books, interspersed with photos and mementos that would otherwise clutter up your desktop. If you don't have room for a free-standing bookcase, consider installing some shelves above work areas with brackets and painted or stained wooden shelves. These can accommodate often-used supplies, manuals, and display mementos as well. Rolling carts can be placed next to your desk, in the closet, or in a corner, depending on the frequency of use. And your desk can be traditional, sturdy metal, modular, or you can create a work table/desk unit by using two two-drawer filing cabinets to support a hollow core door or a piece of laminated or butcher block wood stretched between the two cabinets.

Often the best layout is based on an L- or U-shaped work unit that wraps around so that you don't have to get out of your chair to reach the desktop (work) area, the equipment area, or the project area. Modular work units are generally set up in this manner to begin with, but if you don't want to buy a modular unit, you can do it yourself. Simply start with the desk as the "bottom" of the L and wrap around to the right (if you're right-handed, to the left if you're left-handed) with the equipment stand; and for the U plan, continue around a corner (and directly behind the desk) with a credenza, project table, or rolling cart system.

Portable Organizers

Portable organizers can help keep the paper clutter organized and under control. Look at your papers and office supplies and estimate what you will need in the way of organizers to help you maximize the use of your space and increase efficiency before you shop. Remember that you can benefit from freestanding portable organizers that will sit atop your desk and fit into drawers.

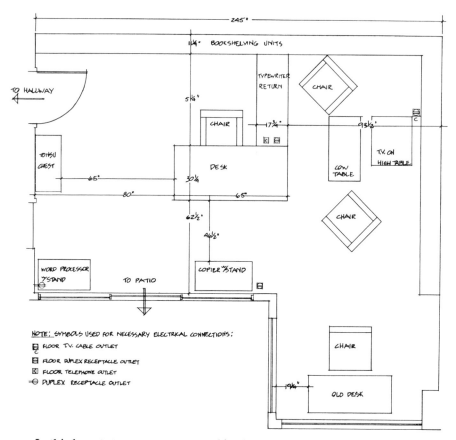

In this layout, two rooms were combined to make one large and sunny office/ sitting area. The space was opened by removing the wall that separated the two rooms, providing space for several people to work when necessary as well as a comfortable sitting area for conferences or TV watching. The main desk "wraps around," with the bookshelves providing arm's-reach storage behind the desk. The position of the desk allows a clear view of the entire layout, the outdoors, and the television.

Space planning and design by Maxine Ordesky, Beverly Hills, California.

PORTABLE ORGANIZERS CHECKLIST

These organizers are nearly always useful, and I recommend everyone have them on hand. (Refer to Part Three, Keeping Paper in Its Place, for other suggestions about paper organizers that might be helpful to you):

☐ *Wire Baskets* — These are great for holding things "to do" and "to pay." Check the size and match it to your legal- or letter-sized format. Also,

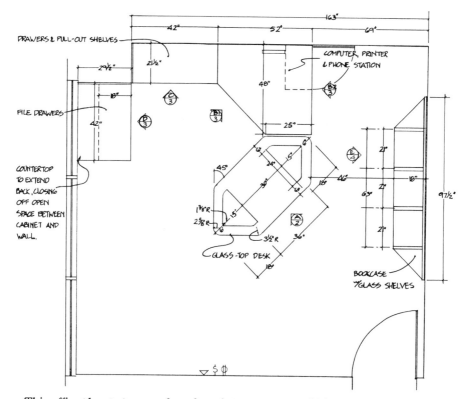

This office plan puts several work and storage areas within arm's reach. The filing cabinet behind the desk features an extra-wide countertop with plenty of room for temporary storage of special project-related paperwork. The empty space under the countertop and between the back of the filing cabinet and the wall is perfect for storing oversized papers and artwork.

Space planning and design by Maxine Ordesky, Beverly, Hills, California.

get a set of posts so you can stack one on top of the other, thus saving space. Whatever you do, resist the temptation to buy smoke-colored lucite or other colored plastic baskets. They offer limited space once they are hooked together, come apart and topple over easily, and in general don't work well.

☐ *Rolling Carts* — These can be used for any number of purposes. Hanging files fit in the top, providing organized storage for project files or for forms and supplies that you need access to often. Baskets at the bottom hold supplies or other oversized items.

☐ *Sweater and Shoeboxes* — These clear plastic boxes, available at variety and closet stores, are great for storing bank statements, photos, and

Make sure your To File basket is roomy enough to collect lots of your "to be filed" papers.

Shu Yamamoto

other out-of-date, bulky records (such as manuscripts or sales materials). These can then be stored on shelves, in cabinets, or under the bed.

☐ *Hot Files* — These lucite bins mount directly onto a wall over your work area (or can be affixed with magnets onto the side of a filing cabinet) and are good for holding records that need to be constantly accessible or for holding small special projects. Although these will accommodate several file folders, they can bear only so much weight, so don't consider them if you plan to keep reams of research at hand.

☐ *Desk Drawer Organizers* — These inexpensive organizers are great for keeping rubber bands, paper clips, pens, pencils, and the like organized inside your desk drawer.

☐ *Drawer Stationery Trays* — These trays drop into a desk drawer and keep stationery organized by providing layered storage that is easy to get to.

☐ *Transfile Boxes* — These sturdy boxes with lids and handle grips are perfect for storing old records. Get several of these.

☐ *Wicker Baskets* — I recommend two large, square wicker baskets — one for things to read and one for things to file. These baskets can go under your desk or next to it, but not *on* it.

SETTING UP YOUR FILES

There are different schools of thought as to the best method for organizing papers and files. The most common methods are filing alphabetically by name, filing by subject, and numeric filing. (I never advocate the numeric system because it involves assigning numbers to files and matching those numbers to an index. This convoluted system is great if you are a spy and don't want anyone to be able to understand your files. You'll have a hard time understanding it *yourself,* since with a numeric system there's no such thing as opening a drawer and immediately seeing the file you need—all you see is a bunch of goofy numbers that are impossible to immediately understand and that require time-consuming indexing.)

The simplest system for keeping your papers organized is to alphabetize them by name. It is a universal system that can be immediately understood by just about anyone who knows his or her ABCs. Using the alphabetical system as the backbone of your paper/filing organization, you can customize your system by grouping certain files into categories first, followed by the subject subtitles (name of file) listed alphabetically. For example, a common category might be *Finances.* A file might read, *Finances* (category) *American Express* (alphabetical subject name). *Warning*: You should only assign a category for an area that generates a lot of files for you. Generally I don't recommend breaking things down by category unless you've got at least a file drawer's worth of papers and files that fall under any one category. Less than that doesn't justify the extra work and thought that inevitably goes into establishing and maintaining extensive categories.

Types of Files

Nevertheless, there are several other types of files you can use to develop your filing system. You probably won't use all of the following files—some of them aren't even recommended—but see which ones will work for you.

Action, Hot, or Working Files. These are files that you need to access every day. Generally, these are kept in your desk file drawer, in a file rack on top of your desk, or in a hot file rack mounted on the wall by your desk. Simply select one title of the three that you like best and think of those daily files as your hot, action, or working files.

Filing Tip: You don't need to write the word "action," "hot," or "working" (depending on the word you choose) on your file. The fact that you store the file in the desk or rack in itself indicates that it is very active. When you don't need these files on a daily basis, simply return them to the permanent files.

Tickler or Suspense Files. These are files that can be kept either in the desk drawer or in a cart next to your desk and are set up so that you have a daily reminder of what needs to be done on that day. For example, if you are an insurance agent, you would need this file so that you would know what policies are up for renewal on any given date. Simply set up file folders (inside hanging folders) that are marked 1 through 31 (one for each day of the month). Behind these put twelve folders, one for each month of the year, January through December. Now if a policy is due to be renewed on the 15th of this month, put it in the folder marked 15. If it is due for renewal on the 15th of, say next month, which is December, put the reminder behind December. When December rolls around, take all of the December papers out of the December file and file them accordingly behind the days of the current month (now this piece of paper would be put in the folder marked 15). In order for this file to work, you do have to check the file religiously every day.

Filing Tip: Although a cart is the best storage device for a tickler file, there are other, creative ways to set up a tickler (or follow-up) file. For example, if you are a salesperson, you can set up a tickler file in a binder to help you keep track of sales prospects (see Sales Prospects in Part Two for more information on how to do this). You may want to set this up in your desk file drawer, which is also fine, as long as you have the room. *Warning:* Don't be tempted to put your tickler or suspense (follow-up) paperwork into an accordion file. Accordion files always look handy dandy, but in reality they are traps for paper. The accordion file quickly becomes stuffed and so bulky that it is difficult to deal with. Also, papers tend to get crammed into this container, resulting in papers that invariably get squashed at the bottom of the section or, worse, accidentally filed behind the wrong tab to begin with. Stick with carts, bins, or binders and leave the accordion folders to other, less serious paper pushers.

Project Files. These are files that pertain to a particular project. For example, you may be writing a book that requires research in several different areas. To keep your materials organized, you'll make up files for the different categories of research as well as files for your notes and drafts. You will be working on these materials on an ongoing basis, so you don't want to integrate these project files into your permanent files just yet. Other project file examples include lawsuits, special university projects, fundraising events, and major deals involving negotiation with several people.

Filing Tip: A rolling cart is perfect for temporary storage of these files (you can hang them in hanging folders across the top of the cart). Often these carts have baskets underneath that give you space for supplies that might go with the project (such as reference magazines or stationery). A spare surface is also handy for those times when you might need to sort and reorganize or hold some of the project materials. This surface can be

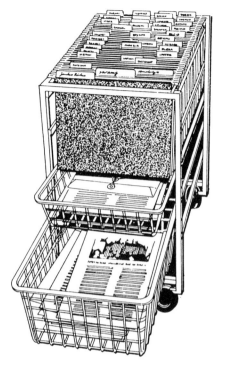

A rolling cart is great for organizing special projects.

Shu Yamamoto

your credenza top or a "project table" (either a portable table that you put up when needed or a table that is a fixed piece of furniture in the room), or it can be the bed in the spare bedroom where your desk is located.

Again, you don't need to write the word "project" on your file, since the fact that you have it stored in the project cart will tell you that it is a project you are working on. When you are finished with the project, simply integrate the files into your permanent filing system or store them in trans-file boxes.

Chronological (or Chron) Files. These are files that are kept, usually in a binder, by chronological date; the paperwork with the most recent date is usually filed on the top. Often the binders are divided by month or, in some cases, by week. These are good for minutes of meetings and for keeping working records pertaining to upcoming events. Many companies also use them for keeping internal correspondence records. At home, these binders can provide an effective way to store children's school papers, with an allocation of one large binder for each school year.

Filing Tip: These binders are convenient for two reasons: They need not be stored in a filing cabinet drawer, thus saving critical interior drawer space (store them on a shelf), and they are very portable, which means that you can easily take them with you to meetings, for example, where you might need to refer to some of the previous meeting records that would now be in the binder.

Permanent Files. These are the alphabetical files that are kept permanently in your filing cabinet for reference when needed.

Filing Tip: Don't take the word "permanent" to heart. You will *not* want to keep these files forever (unless you are a confirmed pack rat, in which case you'll go on storing every scrap of paper that comes into your life, regardless of what I may have to say about it). To help keep those "permanent" files under control, weed out your files at least once or (preferably) twice each year. Another tip is to weed out a file when you have it in front of you. If you are digging through a file and see papers that can be tossed, then toss them right then. What are you waiting for? Of course, when you weed out files, some of the papers and files will get moved to your archival files. But before you do that, and in fact, before you even put a piece of paper into the permanent files in the first place, remember that you will never again look at 80 percent of everything you file.

Archival Files. These are files that you have to keep, for one reason or another, for many years. This generally means papers that are legal or financial in nature. Once these papers have passed their active date (for instance, papers from two years ago) they are best moved to storage so that they don't choke up the daily permanent filing cabinet space. These files can be stored in transfile boxes (available at the office supply store) and stored in another location (such as a storage room, the garage, a closet, or another self-storage unit rented for this purpose).

Filing Tip: Where people go wrong with archival files is when they start dumping instead of deciding. Rather than deciding to get rid of college papers from ten years ago, they get dumped into the archival file boxes. Rather than deciding to get rid of those outdated vendor brochures, they get dumped into the archival file boxes. Rather than deciding to get rid of some of little Johnny's papers from kindergarten (and Johnny is now in college), those papers get dumped in the archival boxes. You get the idea. So decide before you dump. And to further control the files in these archival boxes, mark a destroy date on the file folder and then on the front of the box. Then, when the date rolls around, toss the contents without looking at them. If you want to save some papers that are really mementos, choose just a few: a *small* selection of Johnny's papers; one term paper from each college year rather than all the papers you ever generated over the four years; several of those vendor brochures (aw, c'mon, do you really have to keep those?).

Finally, when you move files into the archival file box, remove the manila folder from the hanging folder and store only the manila folder in the box. You can reuse the hanging folder in your permanent filing cabinet, and you'll save space in the archival boxes. You'll probably never look at those files again in this lifetime anyway (unless, maybe, you move), and hanging folders are awkward in storage boxes.

Pending Files. These are files that people generally keep for matters that are "pending." Usually this is one file folder that is kept in or on the desk. I hate these things, because they're like a black hole. Stuff gets dropped into these files to be blissfully forgotten forever. If you can't figure out what to do with a piece of paper, plop, it goes into Pending. If you really don't want to deal with it now, but tell yourself that you will do it "later," it gets dumped into Pending. If it requires follow-up in the future, again, it goes into Pending. Pending is the file you make up to con yourself into thinking that your unpleasant paper matters are being handled.

Filing Tip: Don't even think of setting up one of these files. They won't help you, and chances are they won't fool anyone else either.

FILING SUPPLY CHECKLIST

You will need the following minimum supplies to set up your new filing system or to clean up an old one:

☐ Third-cut Manila Folders—one box of one hundred

☐ Hanging File Folders—four boxes of twenty-five each. Make sure you get hanging file folders with *clear,* not colored tabs, and make sure the tabs are short two-inch tabs (No. 42 on the box)

☐ File Label Stickers—one box

☐ Extra box of clear (No. 42) plastic tabs for the hanging folders

If you want to set up a chronological file or a sales prospect file, you will also need the following:

☐ Large Binder

☐ One set of Alphabetical Dividers

☐ One set of Dividers marked 1 through 31

☐ One set of Dividers marked with the months of the year

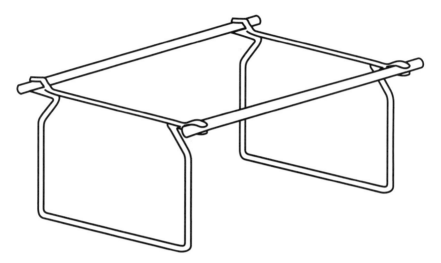

If your filing cabinet doesn't already have rails to accommodate hanging files, you can purchase one for each drawer at your local office supply store. They are inexpensive and easy to assemble and install; they'll turn your cabinet into one that will comfortably hold hanging files.

JBL Graphics, Montrose, California

If you have especially bulky files or need to file computer papers or binders in your filing cabinet, you will also want to buy:

☐ Hanging Box-bottom Folders — One box of twenty-five (These hanging files have extra wide bottoms to accommodate bulky items, such as binders or extra thick reports.)

Finally, to help alphabetize and sort the papers that need to be filed, you should buy:

☐ Alphabetical Sorter — one

You'll want to make sure you always have a sufficient quantity of filing supplies on hand so that setting up new files is convenient. Store your filing supplies near their point of first use — manila folders, hanging file folders, and binders near the file area, and labels near the typewriter.

Creating a New File

Every time you set up a new file, make up two folders, a manila folder *and* a hanging folder.

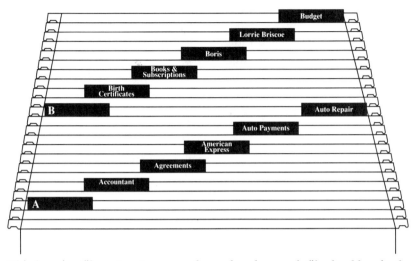

This hanging file system permanently marks where each file should go in the file drawer and makes locating a file fast and easy.

JBL Graphics, Montrose, California

The Manila Folder. This is the folder that will actually house your papers and that you will pull out of the drawer when you need to review some of the paperwork inside (*never* remove the hanging file folder). Before you place any papers into the file, unfold any that are folded and remove all paperwork from envelopes (throw the envelopes away). Throw away any junk, remove paper clips, and staple any paperwork that needs to be kept together. Give some extra thought to anything that is particularly bulky before you file it. Bulky items such as magazines and brochures take up a lot of space quickly, and as a general rule, should not be placed in a file. (For more information on how to store these, see Brochures and Magazines in Part Two.) Put all pertinent papers into the folder in chronological order, with the most recent piece of paper on the top (this makes it easier to find the most current information whenever you access the file). If the file becomes relatively full, you can score the bottom of the folder so that the papers sit well into the file (otherwise the papers in a too full folder will pop up and obscure the identifying tab). To score the file folder, simply bend the folder along one of the creased lines at the bottom.

Type or write a label and affix it to the file tab. If you write rather than type, make sure that both the title you select and your handwriting are very clear. To find the best title for the file, simply pick the words by which you are most likely to remember the contents of the file. For instance, if you have a client named Andrews Plumbing, and you are more likely to remember it under Plumbing, put the word "Plumbing" first, followed by "Andrews." If you are more likely to remember it by the client's name, Andrews, then mark the file with the word "Andrews" first. On the manila folder, it is important to make the title as complete as possible, noting the category and the subject. For example:

CLIENT—ANDREWS PLUMBING
This would be filed in the Client drawer under *A*;
or
CLIENT—PLUMBING, ANDREWS
This would be filed in the Client drawer under *P*.

The Hanging File. The hanging folder is the "jacket" for your real file and is not meant to be removed from the drawer; rather it is meant to serve as a permanent marker for where your file goes when it is returned to the drawer. Your manila folder fits into the hanging file folder, and an identifying label is typed or written to fit into the plastic tab. This eliminates misfiling altogether, and since the plastic tabs stick up in the drawer, it's much easier to locate the file you need at a glance.

The identifying title that you insert into the plastic tab should match the title on the manila folder. These plastic tabs are small; you may have to abbreviate some of your title. Also, it may not be necessary to include the category on this tab if you have allocated an entire drawer to a specific category. For example, if one entire drawer contains only client files, you need only mark Clients on the front of the drawer and include Clients on the manila folder (so that you know at a glance what drawer to return the manila folder to). Since the drawer is already marked, it is not necessary to categorize the hanging file, which is never removed from the drawer. For example:

Manila Folder:	CLIENTS—ANDREWS PLUMBING
Hanging Folder:	ANDREWS PLUMBING
Cabinet Drawer:	CLIENTS

The manila folder would be filed in the Andrews Plumbing hanging jacket under *A* in the Clients drawer.

When you insert the plastic tab into the hanging jacket, make sure you insert it *into the front of the jacket.* One of the advantages of the hanging file system is that it offers you fingertip access to your files, because when you see a plastic tab that identifies the file you want, your fingers automatically touch that tab, which in turn automatically opens the hanging jacket to reveal the folder you need inside. If you put the plastic tab *on the back* of

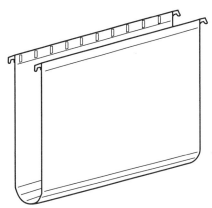

Each hanging file folder marks a permanent place in your filing cabinet for a specific file, effectively eliminating any misfiles. You can score the manila folder along the creased lines at the bottom so it will hold more and sit well in the hanging file folder.

JBL Graphics, Montrose, California

the jacket, your fingers will automatically move you to the file *behind* the one you really want, and you will have to back up to get to the desired file.

The placement of the plastic tab in the drawer can also make a difference. Although some people swear by placing the plastic tabs all flush left or flush right in the drawer, I find that this just ends up frustrating the people who have to work with the files because it is impossible to see the labels without using your fingers to pull the files forward one by one. I prefer to stagger these tabs, starting from left to right, throughout the entire drawer. Then, when the drawer is opened, you really can see all of the files without digging with your fingers to find what you want. As you add new files over the time, you may have to stop every once in a while to reposition the tabs, but this only takes a few minutes. I think it's worth it to save yourself the finger search that you would otherwise have to undertake every time you opened the drawer.

Don't Overstuff Your Files. Be careful not to overstuff your files with papers; it will make it more difficult to find a particular piece of paper because you'll have to sift through just that many more papers, which by now have usually been shuffled around so much that they are out of chronological order. For instance, if you put a thick manila folder into a hanging jacket, it will pop up and obscure the plastic tab, defeating the purpose of the hanging folder, which is to clearly mark where your files are and where they are to be returned when they have been removed from the drawer. You can solve this problem by scoring the bottoms of the hanging jackets whenever necessary. If, for some reason, you need to store exceptionally bulky items or to store more than one file folder (with the same title) in the hanging jacket, and scoring the folder doesn't accommodate the extra bulk, you can use a box-bottom hanging jacket.

Rather than stuffing things into a box-bottom hanging file, it is often better to break down bulky files into separate file folders that can then be stored in a single hanging file folder. You'll find that, overall, the drawer stays neater than when you use a lot of box-bottom hanging files to hold overstuffed or multiple file folders. Here are some examples of how you can break down bulky files into separate files that can then be stored in their own hanging file folder:

FINANCIAL — American Express — Jan-June 1990
FINANCIAL — American Express — July-Dec 1990
CLIENTS — ABC Contracting — Correspondence 1990
CLIENTS — ABC Contracting — Orders 1990

If you are working on filing a large backlog, you can speed the process up a bit with the help of an alphabetical sorter (available at stationery stores). Once a file is set up, make sure that the collection of papers inside the folder is in chronological order, so that retrieval of the most current paperwork is easy and logical.

Regular Elimination Makes for Healthy Files. You may want to label your files when you set them up so that you will know at a glance when to store or to destroy the file. Although I don't recommend numeric filing or color coding, you may want to use a very *simple* color code or numeric system to automatically call your attention to files that are ready to be stored or destroyed. Marking the year's date (use the last two digits — as in 90 for 1990) in large colored letters can help you weed out files if they become dated automatically. For example, all of your 1990 files might have a large, red 90 on them; 1991's would sport a large yellow 91 on them; and 1992's would have a green 92. Your eye would easily pick up the 1990 files in 1991 or 1992 and would let you know, depending on the nature of the files, when to remove them from the current/active system. Even with color-coded numbers, you'll want to make sure you go through the papers in the file before you toss or store it, since you can never tell when you might happen upon a misfiled item you thought was lost forever. All of this fancy numeric tagging and color coding is unnecessary if you'll just go through your files routinely every six to twelve months. You can make your store/destroy decisions then on the spot—and you'll have spared yourself the expense and extra effort that those special colored and/or numbered labels require.

FILING CATEGORIES CHECKLIST

Here are some categories that you may want to use for your filing system:

☐ Business   ☐ Legal

☐ Clients   ☐ Personal

☐ Financial   ☐ Real Estate

☐ General   ☐ Reference Resource

Allocate filing drawer space according to your needs. For example, you may need one entire drawer for your Financial files, but you may be able to store both your General and Reference/Resource files in one drawer that you've divided in half.

FILING SUBJECT CHECKLIST

Here are some subject headings that you may want to use within the main categories of your filing system:

BUSINESS:

☐ Accounts Payable

☐ Accounts Receivable

☐ Correspondence

☐ Expenses

☐ General Information

☐ Suppliers/Vendors

CLIENTS:

☐ (List alphabetically by client name)

FINANCIAL:

☐ **Auto**
Gasoline
Payments
Registration
Repairs

☐ **House**
Improvements
Inventory
Mortgage
Repairs

☐ **Insurance**
Auto (or file under Auto)
Health
House
Life

☐ **Investments**
Pension Plan
Savings
Stocks and Bonds

☐ **Medical**

☐ **Receipts**
American Express
Department Stores
MasterCard
Miscellaneous
Office Supplies
Petty Cash
Postage
Visa

☐ **Social Security**

☐ **Taxes**
Information
Return (note year)
Return Backup Information
(note year)

☐ **Utilities**
Gas
Electricity
Telephone
Water

GENERAL:

☐ Children's Records
(subdivide by child)

☐ Correspondence

☐ Health Information

☐ Pet Records

☐ Product Information

☐ Warranties and Instructions

PERSONAL:

☐ Birth Certificate

☐ Career Information

☐ Correspondence

☐ Family History

☐ Resumes

☐ School Transcript

☐ Will

LEGAL:

File alphabetically by case name; keep all records in strict chronological order; separate expenses. For example:

Culp vs. Anderson
Culp vs. Anderson — Expenses

Major cases will require that records be divided into several different files according to the nature of the document.

REAL ESTATE:

☐ File by property location. For example;

Miami Condo
3824 Ocean View Blvd.

Prescott Cabin

New York Apartment
208 W. 23rd St.

(File alphabetically)

REFERENCE/RESOURCE:

☐ Affirmations

☐ Art

☐ Articles

☐ Cartoons and Humor

☐ Children's Activities

☐ Decorating Ideas

☐ Dentists

☐ Doctors

☐ Family History (Genealogy)

☐ House Repair Services

☐ Local Professional Services

☐ Restaurants

☐ Travel

This category is the best place for you to set up any reference/resource files that you may need for your hobby or special interest.

The Master File

Although I am generally against indexing, I think it can be a good idea to set up a Master file for emergency purposes. This file would let a member of your family or a colleague know where to find certain critical documents in the event that something happened to you. For example, your personal Master file might include information on where your family can locate the following documents:

Banking Records

Birth Certificate

Burial Arrangements or Instructions

Citizenship Papers

Disaster Recovery Plan

Insurance Policies

Investment Records

Marriage Certificate

Military Discharge and Veterans Records

Pension or Retirement Information

Power of Attorney

Safety Deposit Box Information

Social Security Records

Tax Records

Titles or Deeds

Will

Make a list of where all of these papers can be found, and note all pertinent account numbers in this Master file. You may want to keep copies of some of the records in this file (such as the Power of Attorney), with the originals in a safety deposit box. A fireproof filing cabinet or fireproof box can also be a good idea, particularly where there is a lot of documentation (lots of investments, for example). Keep your Master file in a fireproof box or file it under *M* in your filing cabinet.

Tell your family about the file, and let them know exactly where it is. This way you won't have to explain to them where every file is; the Master file location is all they need to know. If something happens to you, they'll bless you for organizing this paperwork in advance for them, saving them lots of additional headache and heartache.

Disaster Recovery Plan

While a Master file can be invaluable as a resource for others, an even more important consideration is what paperwork you would need in the event of a disaster. In the event of a natural disaster, such as fire, flood, hurricane, tornado, or earthquake, certain types of paperwork may be needed immediately in order to function effectively in the aftermath of the disaster. A Master file won't solve your problems, which will no doubt be overwhelming during and after the disaster. Assume, for the moment, that an unexpected natural disaster has struck your home or office. Now ask yourself the following questions:

- If your home or office were condemned, and you had only fifteen minutes to retrieve all of your belongings, what would you grab?

- If all of your records were destroyed, how would you identify yourself?

- How would you get access to funds at the bank with no identification, and how would you prove the extent of your holdings there?

- How would you process an insurance claim with your insurance company with no identification to prove who you are?

- How would you facilitate hospital treatment with no insurance card or other identification?

- With no immediate identifiction, how could you be sure you could gain access to property of yours that has been cordoned off?

- How will you replace one-of-a-kind records pertaining to your family history?

- How will you reconstruct your credit card holdings, and how will you verify your current balances?

- If you own your own business, could you continue business or even rebuild your business if you lost all of your records?

- How would you claim property such as your car or furnishings, or even your home, without documentation to prove that you are the owner, and what would happen to that property in an unsettled social climate if it took you thirty days or longer to prove ownership?

- If you lose all of your records and identification, and a close relative dies in the disaster, how will you prove that s/he is your relative (this proof will be necessary to facilitate burial arrangements and to process claims against that person's immediate estate or belongings). And if you die and your will is destroyed in the disaster, how will your beneficiaries ever have the access to your estate that you have deemed appropriate?

• Once the disaster has passed and things return to normal, what methods will you use to compile and file your tax return, and what will you use for substantiation?

Given that the recovery from a natural disaster can take some time, it stands to reason that if you lose all of your records pertaining to your assets and insurance, you can count on intensifying the aggravation and anguish of your personal and professional recovery at least tenfold.

To prepare yourself, you may want to initiate a Disaster Recovery Plan for your records. Gather all of your most important documents and copy them so that you can have one set of records in another location. You will want to be able to identify yourself as soon as possible after the disaster, and then you will want to be able to lay claim and identify your property that may have been damaged or destroyed. The following checklist can give you an idea of some of the records that you may want to duplicate and store elsewhere for disaster recovery purposes:

DISASTER RECOVERY PLAN CRITICAL RECORDS CHECKLIST

☐ Birth Certificate

☐ Marriage License

☐ Social Security Number (Card)

☐ Military Discharge Records

☐ Driver's License

☐ Car Registration

☐ Car Pink Slip (Ownership Documentation)

☐ Medical Insurance Identification Card and Policy

☐ Homeowners Insurance Policy

☐ Auto Insurance Identification Card and Policy

☐ Life Insurance Policy

☐ Bank Checking Account Numbers

☐ Bank Savings Account Numbers

☐ Investment Records Documentation (such as Stock Certificates, Certificates of Deposit, and IRA Accounts)

☐ Deeds

☐ Family Historical Information and/or Photos

☐ Critical Address/Mailing Lists

☐ Tax Returns (for at least the previous five years, with appropriate back-up records for substantiation)

☐ Business Records Required to Survive or Rebuild

☐ Will

The location you pick for storage of duplicate records is up to you. Some people think that a fireproof box or safe is sufficient, and in most cases, it is. But this method of storage assumes that you will be able to *get to* that box or safe immediately after the disaster. In the case of an earthquake, for example, it may be impossible to get near your house (if it is still standing), and even if you can, identification may be required to enter the area. A safety deposit box in a bank is good, but again, in an earthquake the bank may be destroyed. In the event of massive destruction, often the best answer is to have records stored in another city or state. Major businesses generally rely on a back-up system stored in another city, and you might want to consider that as well. You can put the records in a safety deposit box or a self-storage unit, or store them at a relative's house in your other location; hopefully, they will be out of the disaster area and will have a full set of records for you, thus saving you the months it would otherwise take to reestablish your holdings and identification.

Whatever you decide (based on your area's particular weather/environmental potential for disaster), implementing your own personal Disaster Recovery Plan may be the most important organizing you will ever do in your life.

Since You Asked Me . . .

When you set up or clean out your files and piles of papers, there will probably be lots of things you think you should do. Somehow it just comes to you, for example, that you should color code everything. Or that you *need* a bulletin board. Other things will require decisions or choices, such as choosing letter-sized or legal-sized cabinets and filing supplies. You may not know for sure which is best, or you may think you know what's best but could still be talked out of it.

In my experience with people and their papers, I've found that the same choices come up for discussion and dispute time and time again. Here are some of those questions and attitudes, along with what I think of them:

Should I Use Letter- or Legal-Sized Cabinets and Filing Supplies?
Well, that depends. If you've got money to burn and space to spare, well,
hey, why not go legal? It takes up much more space and costs a lot more
money, but, gee, when that one legal document comes in, you'll be able to
file it, nice and flat, with no problem. If, on the other hand, money and
space are a concern, then I advise people to always go with letter-sized
unless more than 40 percent of their paperwork is legal-sized. You can fold
the bottom of a legal document so that it fits into a letter-sized folder, and
although this adds a little unwanted bulk to the drawer, it is more cost and
space efficient in the long run to do it this way if the majority of your
paperwork is letter-sized.

Do I Really Need to Buy Those Hanging Folders? Well, you don't *have*
to do anything. Lots of people don't want to buy these folders because they
are expensive, and in the end they do take up extra room in the file drawer,
and I agree with both of those assessments. But I do think the time you
save is more than worth the expense. These hanging folders mark the
permanent place where any given file can be located at any time, so you
won't have to spend time digging for a file that has been accidentally misfiled behind something else. These files put an end to paper cuts and hang-
nails that invariably result from constant pawing through manila file folders
to find what you are looking for. And all the news is not bleak; they are
easy to reuse and should last a virtual lifetime. When a file is tossed or
moved to storage, you can simply remove the manila folder file, type a new
insert for the plastic tab on the hanging file, and use it anywhere you like
in your filing system.

Wouldn't Color Coding Be a Neat Idea? Not by me, it wouldn't. Color
coding just means double work. Before you can make a file, you have to
stop and think, What color folder does this get? Then you have to make
sure you actually have such a colored folder on hand. More often than not,
you find yourself out of a particular color, so papers don't get filed because
they are waiting for their *color,* for cripe's sake. And if you've got four
or five colors going, it gets downright confusing. Plus you've guaranteed
yourself the job of file clerk for life, because it's a sure bet that nobody
else will ever be able to decipher, on a regular basis, your cockeyed color
system.

Won't We Need an Index to Help Us Locate the Files? I hope not. I'd much rather see you use the KISS rule—Keep It Simple, Stupid. When people start talking about indexes, I start thinking complicated, and in my mind, life is complicated enough already. Any way you look at it, once you open a filing cabinet drawer, you have to *look* for the file you want. With an index, first you *look* at the index, then you do what you'd have to do anyway—you open the drawer and *look* for the file. So that's an extra step. And every time you add a file or remove a file to storage, the index has to be changed, so now you're really looking at some extra work. Unless you've got rooms-full of filing cabinets, I'm against an index. And even if you've got rooms full, I think a *map* is a better idea. It can just get you to the right room; after that, the KISS rule kicks in.

Shouldn't I Cross-reference Some of My Files? Only if it's legally necessary. Otherwise, I'm against cross-referencing for two basic reasons. One, it's more work and can create confusion (creating questions as to *which* of two files, for example, a piece of paper should go into). And two, unless you are in the middle of a research project that requires this method of tracking information (and if you are, I hope it's only temporary, because you've probably got too much paper), you are storing too much paper. Cross-referencing in the files can be looked on as duplication in a sense. Why not put everything in *one* file or put everything in a few files located in the same spot and save yourself all of that noting, checking, and looking. And I'd be willing to bet that once you put all the papers together, bypassing indexing, you'll discover needless duplication of information.

Won't a Bulletin Board Be a Good Idea to Help Me Remember Important Phone Numbers and Dates? No, a thousand times, no. If you want to clutter up your life with a hanging paper burial ground, get a bulletin board. Then do what everyone else does with it; start sticking things up there that you either "need" or like to look at. Initially you tell yourself that you will stick (and *stick* is the key word here) critical I-need-to-be-reminded-of-this items on the board. This visual tickler system soon evaporates as you find yourself automatically impaling postcards from Europe (sent to you by Aunt Clara), cartoons that are especially politically significant to your life and times, telephone numbers, and assorted schedules on the board. You find yourself operating most of the time with a shortage of tacks and pushpins, and before you know what happened, the board is loaded with pieces of paper, one crucified on top of another, making the whole mess a vertical paper burial ground that ultimately leaves you with an obnoxiously non-functional eyesore. The bulletin board is the ultimate receptor for postponed decisions. After all, where should you *put* that post-

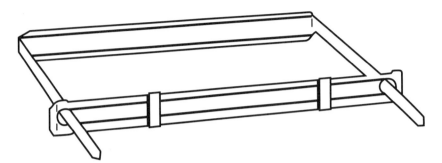

Although not generally recommended, fasteners can be helpful in keeping certain types of files orderly, such as insurance claims.

JBL Graphics, Montrose, California

card and cartoon? You can't figure it out, so up it goes, on the bulletin board. Now, when you can't figure it out, look it up in Part Two of this book. Things typically found on the average bulletin board that are covered in this book are Postcards, Phone Numbers, Schedules, and Tickets. Remember, you've got enough paper clutter without hanging it on the wall.

Don't I Need to Use Those Fasteners to Lock My Papers Down In the File Folders? This one gets mixed reviews. As with so many good ideas, this one requires extra work, and I am always against extra work. These fasteners are great because they keep the papers in the file in the order that you want them. Insurance brokers and lawyers, for example, seem to be locked into this way of securing papers in their files. If several people are rummaging through the files with regularity, and it seems like they are always making a mess of the papers inside each file, then these fasteners can help impose a little discipline. A person might think twice before removing the fastener to dig down two thirds of the way in a file to pull out a piece of paper just to read it. They'll read it without pulling it out. Which is good. Very good. On the other hand, if the paper has to be pulled out of the file for some reason, it is unlikely that this person will then go to the trouble of carefully putting the paper back in the file, two thirds of the way down and then carefully lining up the holes of all the other papers so that those papers can be positioned correctly to be clamped back down with the fastener. Then there's the matter of punching holes in originals (such as policies) so they can be fastened down. You're not supposed to do that. Yet some people forget and do just that, they're so danged hole happy. I dunno. I think an organized file with these things looks fabulous. But I never recommend using them. Because in the long run I don't think they solve any problems, and they are just too much *work.*

Wouldn't It Be a Good Idea to Use Accordion Files for Some of My

Project Files or for Some Pending Files? Grrrrr. No. One of the first things I always do when I walk into a client's office is to locate and eliminate the accordion files. Generally, these monsters are in cabinets, on the floor, and spilling over on top of the desk. While the concept of a divided accordion file is a viable one, the reality is that they quickly become impractical. It doesn't take very long for the thing to become overstuffed. Then you start *cramming* (as opposed to normal *stuffing*) papers into this thing. The result? Papers actually get *crumpled* and pushed to the bottom as other papers are stuffed in. The crumpled, wadded papers are gone, trampled to death by other papers. The bigger this file gets, the less inclined you are to look at it. So it gets moved around, generally landing in some dark corner, on the floor, where it becomes a yawning archival file, taking up space and gathering dust, its information, for all practical purposes, gone forever. I don't like'em, never have. They're nothing but a paper trap.

Well, O.K., Then How About Those Nifty Divided File Folders? Can I Use Them for Some Division Within a File? Well, here's another good idea that looks fabulous but gives me pause. People use these, for example, for their insurance paperwork so that they can put all of their different paperwork into one file in an organized manner. Which is great. The problem is, you need to use fasteners to really keep things divided, and I don't much care for fasteners, as I've already said. And I'm not sure that it isn't easier to keep paperwork divided by simply putting the material in separate files. After all (for example) how often do you really look at all of your insurance paperwork — say, auto, health, and house policies? And if you do look at it all at once, wouldn't it be just as easy to pull those three files, since they'll all be filed in the same place in the drawer under Insurance? Finally, you can lead a horse to water, but you can't make him or her drink. Let's face it, it's a human being who takes papers in and out of files. That divided file is not going to *make* you put papers back in the right place, now is it? In fact, you are — I think — more likely to *misfile* something behind the divider in one large file than you are to misfile something into a completely separate file.

Retrieval, or How to Find Papers Once They've Been Filed

One of the biggest problems with papers that have been filed seems to be the "black hole" syndrome. Once something goes into the file, it might just as well have disappeared into a black hole because nobody ever seems to know what happened to said papers or file. If you're not careful, this can even happen to the papers that are filed into your newly set-up or organized filing system. Assuming your filing system is organized and logical, here are some tips to help you and anyone who files papers into the system avoid the black hole:

Be Consistent. Be consistent when you set up new files by selecting titles that conform to the system.

Avoid Duplication. Check periodically to make sure you don't have duplications in the filing cabinet. For example, you might find that you have a file marked Insurance—Health (filed under *I*) and one marked Health Insurance (filed under *H*), thus scattering your records into two totally separate files. Eliminate these duplications by consolidating into one file, and make sure you check the files quickly on a regular basis so you can nip this problem in the bud.

Never, Ever, Remove the Hanging File Folder. This folder permanently marks the correct (alphabetical) spot in the drawer for the papers to be filed. Remove this, and you invite misfiling by someone in too big a hurry to actually stop and *think* about the alphabet as they shove the file back into the drawer.

Don't Let Your Filing Pile Up. Filing is right up there with ironing in terms of satisfaction and personal pleasure. Nevertheless, just like ironing, it needs to be done frequently, just to keep things looking and running smoothly. If you wait until the To File pile is about to run you out of your office, you'll hate the several hours it takes to do the filing, and therefore, you won't pay attention, and you're sure to stuff at least a few papers into the black hole.

Remember That People Aren't Mind Readers. If someone else does your filing for you, it can be wise to remember that that person is not a mind reader. How someone else thinks a paper should be filed may not be the same as how you think it should be filed, but since others cannot read your mind on this, chances are good that they'll do the independent, resourceful thing—file it themselves where they think it *should* be filed. Makes sense to them, but it's the black hole to you. All of which is fine if your filing assistant is always there to get the paper when you need it. The minute that person isn't around, of course, is when you need that piece of paper or file. And it's in the black hole. To eliminate this mind-reader mindset, simply make it a point to remember to mark your papers before you give them to another person for filing. Make a quick note either directly on the piece of paper or on a Post-it attached to the paper that tells how you want it filed. For example, Insurance — Health. Or, if it is a letter from someone, you can circle directly on the paper the information you want it filed under. For example, you may have a letter from Ann Walker at ABC Health Insurance. You could circle Walker on the letter if that is how you want it filed; or you could circle Insurance if that is how you want it filed. Your assistant will then file it where you want it rather than into the black hole. It's a simple solution, and it only takes a few extra seconds as you pass the paper along to implement this small preventative measure.

File Papers Chronologically. File papers chronologically with the most recent paperwork on top. This saves digging through the entire file to find something that was documented yesterday.

Make Sure Your Filing System Is Organized and Up to Date. Take the time to weed through the filing system regularly so that you can move archival records to storage, throw away records that are no longer necessary to keep, and reorganize anything that needs some refining. Do this at least once or twice a year, and you should be able to keep your paper monster at bay.

PAPERS ON THE GO

Keeping paperwork organized in the car or when you travel to other cities is yet another challenge in this paper-pushing world. Some simple steps can help you keep on top of your paperwork as you go.

Car. If you work out of your car, you can put your papers in a portable file bin made expressly for traveling paper organization. These sturdy bins will hold hanging folders and manila files, and many have a tray on top to hold small office supplies, like pens, pencils, and paper clips. You should include files marked To Do, To Pay, To File, and To Read so that you can sort this stuff as you accumulate it. You may also want to add a file marked Calls to Make (when you get back to the office). And you'll probably want one for Expenses, too. The bin will hold them all, and then some. It has a lid with a handle that snaps shut when you don't need to use it, and it is the answer to keeping paper from taking over your rolling office — your car.

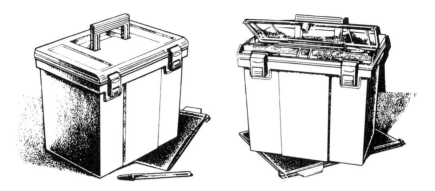

The Box Office® and Large File by Rubbermaid are perfect for portable storage of records.

Box Office® is a registered trademark of Rubbermaid Incorporated, Wooster, Ohio 44691.

Briefcase. To say ahead of paper problems in your briefcase, simply set up the standard four files—To Do, To Pay, To Read, and To File. As you travel, simply put your papers in these files (which I think serve you best when they are kept upright in the pocket that is usually on the inside of most briefcase lids).

If you don't want to carry four separate files for To Do, To Pay, To Read, and To File, you can consolidate the categories into one heavy-duty divided classification file folder with the sections labeled accordingly. You can also add a large mailing envelope marked Expenses, which can be the repository for all of your expense receipts as you travel. (Women may want to carry a business-sized envelope in their purse for this purpose as well.)

If you don't use a briefcase and prefer to travel with a soft-sided bag of some sort, you can keep your files from getting crushed by setting them into a heavy-duty file pocket. These pockets have sides so that papers don't fall out and expand to hold several files as well as paper and envelopes. They are easily transportable and work well as portable file/work stations on the road and in your hotel room.

Doing it on the Road. When you travel, don't forget to carry a supply of postage and mailing envelopes along with a small supply of postcards, stationery, or forms that you might use. Keep the stationery in a file folder so that it stays neat, and use it when you can to send things out as you need to, rather than waiting until you get back to the office.

The most valuable thing you can do to keep yourself and your papers organized when you travel is to use overnight mail services. Express Mail your notes, dictation, even things to be filed, to your office so they can be worked on *while* you are on the road, not *after* you get back. Have your office Express to you all incoming paper matters that need your attention so that you can work on them in the evenings. Time spent in hotel rooms usually lacks the normal office interruptions and phone calls. A couple of hours per evening in a hotel devoted to paperwork can result in twice the paper progress you would be able to make in between crises and phone calls at the office. You'll be rewarded for your on-the-road work and Express-Mail efforts. When you get back to the office you won't have to deal with a mountain of accumulated mail and paperwork.

One final tip: It can make all the difference in the world to stay at hotels that cater to business travelers. It's worth the extra dollars to have access to copying, secretarial, and fax services, so when you book your reservations, ask about the availability of these services.

TRAVELING OFFICE SUPPLY CHECKLIST

These basic supplies will help you keep your papers organized on the road:

- ☐ Large Envelope Marked Expenses

- ☐ File Folders (marked To Do, To Pay, To Read, To File and To Call)

- ☐ File Folders (blank, for setting up new files as you go)

- ☐ Forms (if you use them)

- ☐ Notepad

- ☐ Overnight Mailing Supplies

- ☐ Mailing Envelopes (large manila ones)

- ☐ Paper Clips

- ☐ Paper Punch (small single-hole)

- ☐ Pens, Pencils

- ☐ Postcards

- ☐ Postage

- ☐ Recorder for Dictating

☐ Stationery and Envelopes

☐ Stapler (small)

☐ Staple Remover

STAYING ON TOP OF PAPER

Besides sorting papers immediately and filing records sensibly, these tips can help you forestall future paper clutter and possible paper-noia:

Decide to Decide. Make a commitment to making decisions about your paperwork. Stop putting papers in piles "just for now" because you can't make a decision about what to do with them. Decide to read it, file it, pay it, or do it. Then, *do it.*

Do It Now. To ensure that you don't let your To Do basket become a burial ground, start each day by going through the box and prioritizing what needs to be done. If some of the projects are long-term ones, and especially if you find yourself procrastinating repeatedly by not doing those particular projects in your basket, you might have to pencil in on your calendar exactly *when* you are going to spend time on that project in your To Do file that you have, up to now, been avoiding. Then, *do it.*

Out in the Open. Never keep any work in progress inside your desk drawers. All work in progress should go into the To Do or To Pay baskets or in the special project cart or area. Thus, work not yet finished won't become buried (or lost) in a drawer somewhere, and you will be able to tell at a glance the amount of work yet to be done or the status of work currently in progress.

Make Time. Set aside a regular time to pay bills, do the filing, and read. You'll stay ahead of the paper piles if you do.

Copycat. Resist the urge to copy everything you have on paper. Only copy papers that require duplication, such as legal or financial paperwork that is being sent out. Every time you duplicate something on a photocopy machine, you're contributing to the blizzard of papers blanketing the human race.

Final Fifteen. Make sure you spend fifteen minutes at the end of each day tidying up your work area and prioritizing the work you need to do the following day. It helps to clear your head a bit when you put everything in its place once each day. When you hit the paper decks the following day, you'll feel that you are making a fresh start on your paperwork and on the day.

PART TWO

PAPER FROM A TO Z

*An alphabetical listing of specific
paper problems and their solutions.*

Accounts Payable. Accounts Payable is a phrase that actually means Bills or Expenses. For advice on how to handle this paperwork, see Bills and Expenses; simply substitute the words "Accounts Payable" for either of those two words ("Bills" or "Expenses") and use the same filing methods. Additionally, if you use words like "accounts payable," then you've probably got a whole lot of bills to pay that need careful attention by at least one and maybe even a few employees. This being the case, you need a bookkeeping system to keep track of everything, and then, of course, you need a bookkeeper or an accountant or both or several of each. Then I suppose you'll want to get all of these accounts payable computerized. When you do that you can probably fire half of the bean counters in your firm, and then when your cash flow is nil and you miss a payment to a major supplier, you can do what everybody else does; blame it on the *computer.*

Accounts Receivable. Accounts Receivable is a much happier phrase than is accounts payable, as it translates "money that is owed you." Yippee! Depending on the nature of your business, your client base, the size of your business, and its dollar volume, there are any number of methods that can be set up to keep track of the paperwork. When your client is billed, you can use statements that have several carbonized copies; send the original to the client and put a copy into an active Accounts Receivable file that you keep on or near your desk. When your client pays the bill, pull the copy of the statement from your Accounts Receivable file, mark it paid and note the date, then file that copy into the client's file or, if you don't maintain separate client files, file it into an Accounts Receivable — Paid file. (These paid files can be broken down either by month or alphabetically.)

This basic system is only an entry-level method of tracking accounts receivable. Naturally, if you have a thriving business with a broad client base that generates income in vast amounts, then you will need a much more sophisticated system. Once you reach the point where the beginner's paper organizing system is not enough, your best bet is to consult your bookkeeper and/or your accountant.

These professionals can steer you in the right direction and set up an appropriate system to keep track of your receivables, paid or unpaid. Even so, you would do well to remember that no system is written in stone, so if your accountant insists on implementing a system that you don't understand and therefore don't like, require that it be modified until it is easy to understand. You need to know at a glance what your income, your potential income, and your cash flow is at any given moment. Work together with your accounting people until you can agree on a system that serves you and the people who have to process the paperwork and payments for you.

These records should be moved to storage once each year. Chances are you can throw some records away at the end of the year, since your deposits are records of your income. But don't toss anything without first checking with your accountant, or it could come back to haunt you via the IRS.

Addresses. (See Business Cards, Phone Numbers.)

Agendas. (See Meeting Records.)

Announcements. Announcements and invitations all too often get lost in the general incoming mail cluttter. Before you know what happened, you've missed that art gallery opening or that wedding shower that you wanted to attend. Weeks after the event, you come across the announcement or invitation only to find yourself staring stupidly at it, annoyance mounting at having missed the event altogether. To avoid repeating this performance, open your mail when it comes in the door and make your decision about the event on the spot. Check your calendar, and if you have the time available and want to attend the event, mark it on the calendar. (If you're having trouble finding the time to get things done and do what you want to do — like accepting this invitation — try reading my book, *How to Get Organized When You Don't Have the Time.*) Put the announcement (or invitation) either in the back of your calendar if you have a desk calendar (highly recommended) or in a basket under the calendar if you have a wall calendar. When the date rolls around, simply pull out the announcement so that you have all of the pertinent details and directions at hand. Now take a shower, comb your hair, and *go.*

Articles. (See also Resources.) Articles get cut out because they are "interesting," funny, or in perfect alignment with our own brilliant thought processes. They get saved even though they are never read again. They even get (horrors!) photocopied and mailed to other people so that they can share our thrill in these words of wisdom. Eventually, they get filed where they, quite simply, rot. I say read it and weep. Or laugh. Or congratulate yourself on agreeing with the writer of the article. Whatever. Then throw it away.

If tossing the article is unthinkable (for whatever "I might need it someday" reasoning you may be entertaining), then just file it under articles. If you keep so many articles that they are in categories (such as, for instance, articles on education, child care, business practice), then you will want to file them under the category (e.g., under "Education Articles"). If you've got dozens of categories that you insist on keeping organized separately

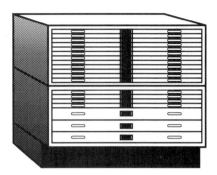

This cabinet provides ideal storage for large pieces of paper or artwork that needs to be stored flat.

JBL Graphics, Montrose, California

(even though you probably never refer to these articles), then you probably need to set up a Research section in your files where you can house all of those articles, alphabetically by category. All in all, it is a lot simpler to do what I suggested in the first place; read it and toss it.

Artwork. Artwork, such as sketches and the like, presents a storage challenge, more than anything. Generally oversized, or at least awkwardly sized, these papers can drift from surface to surface looking for a permanent place to reside. Storing artwork in a filing cabinet can unnecessarily choke up the cabinet and deprive you of space that might otherwise be used for important records and documents. Art supply stores sell cabinets to hold artwork, but these cabinets can be expensive. A little imagination can provide an alternate solution. There's always under the bed as a storage solution (albeit a dusty one), or you can store rolled art in clean, large circular trash cans or in an architect's bin (these bins are great, but expensive). To store large flat pieces, you can adapt a cabinet that you already have by adding plywood partitions to make slots to slide the large pieces into for storage. Or you can take a small bookcase and turn it on end to change it from a horizontal storage unit for books to a vertical storage unit for art. Finally, just because you are a creative genius, you don't have to keep every original work of art that you have put to paper. If it is so great, sell it, hang it on your own walls, or (be careful here) give it to a friend or relative.

Association and Club Records. If you belong to an association or club, chances are that you have more papers about the group than you'll ever need or maybe even read. Tackle the quantity first by quickly perusing the material as soon as it comes in and throwing away all but the most pertinent information. If you belong to several associations, you will need at least one file for Association Dues, so that you can keep track of which association has been paid and of when you will have to renew your dues. You may want to keep this file in your financial drawer (if you have all of your financial files separated into a category apart) since it does involve the payment of money and the possibility of a tax deduction, depending on the type of association and your line of work. Other association and club records can include Board of Directors' minutes and agendas (for information on this, see Meeting Records), newsletters, announcements, and information packets. If you feel obligated to keep a goodly portion of this stuff, consider putting it in three-ring binders rather than choking up your filing cabinet with it all. Make sure you weed out the binders on a regular basis by setting time limits for yourself. For example, you won't need to keep more than six months' worth of newsletters, so once every six months weed out your newsletter binder. Some of you will no doubt dispute this six month theory, saying emphatically that you do too *need* these newsletters more than six months. That being the case, perhaps you should apply for a grant. Because now you're starting a library, and from what I hear, libraries need all the help they can get.

Automobile Records. It's amazing how much paperwork accrues with the ownership of a car. This gets even more complicated in families where there is more than one car. If the paperwork is not kept in good order, your neglect can rise up to haunt you when you try to sell or repair the car. So set up at least one file folder for each car. You may then want to break it down further, depending on the frequency of activity and amount of paperwork on each car. Possible files for keeping track of your automobile paperwork include:

Auto – Gas

Auto – Insurance

Auto – Purchase and Registration

Auto – Repairs

You may want to set up some or all of the files listed above, or you might want to put the gas and insurance files in other areas. With the label Insurance – Auto (car insurance papers could be filed in the same part of the drawer as the other Insurance files). The gasoline bills might be filed under the name of the particular gasoline company, such as Chevron, and filed either alphabetically under *C,* or filed alphabetically in your financial section (since it involves monthly payables).

Another option is to use the word Car instead of Auto, if you are more comfortable with it, and if you have more than one car, you will want to note on the file which car the file refers to. For example, let's say you have two cars, a Ford and a Toyota. You might want to set up separate files for each car:

Car Ford—Gas	Car Toyota—Gas
Car Ford—Insurance	Car Toyota—Insurance
Car Ford—Purchase and Registration	Car Toyota—Purchase and Registration
Car Ford—Repairs	Car Toyota—Repairs

However you set up your files, whether you use Car or Auto and whether or not you put them all together or put some of them in other alphabetical areas (such as the Insurance paperwork), make sure you weed the files regularly. You don't need to keep expired car insurance policies, and you don't need to keep the registration that has expired from years past. And when you sell or total the car, you can get rid of all the paperwork by either giving it to the new owner or throwing it all away. Of course, then you'll probably have to use the files for the next car you own. If you'd move to a city with mass transportation, you could give up the car and all of this paperwork.

Bank Statements. I think bank statements should be kept in their envelopes with the checks. Mark the month and year on the front of the envelope and store the whole business for the year in a storage box from the office supply store or a plastic sweater box (which you can get at a variety store). You can put the box on a shelf, in the closet, under the bed, or in a credenza or cabinet. Many people disagree with my system. They think the thing to do is to remove the statement from the envelope and store it flat in a file folder. The checks are then pulled out and sorted into categories by disbursement. I think that's asking for trouble. I don't know about you, but I'd lose some checks for sure, and since you almost never have to go back to statements or checks anyway unless there's a problem, why go to all that extra effort? Pick your own poison here. If you are ever audited (perish the thought!) you will need these records intact and preferably in good order. Check with the IRS and with your CPA to determine how many years you should keep these records before you toss them.

Bills. Bills, often known also as bad news, need to be handled in an organized manner, since the longer you wait to face up to the news that these bills bring, the greater your chances of compounding what could be a major problem. Burying bills in a pile and telling yourself that they can wait indefinitely is *not* a good idea. That attitude results in shut-down utilities, credit closed at the most inopportune and embarrassing moments, and hostile calls from bill collectors.

Ideally, bills should be paid when they come in. If this were done, they wouldn't pile up and become lost or ignored with disastrous results. Even if you can't pay your bills the minute they arrive, it is important to *open* them immediately. Throw out the junk inserts, clip the return envelope to the bill (do *not* put the bill back into the original envelope — you'll just have to unfold it again), and put the bill in your To Pay basket. At least once every two weeks, check your To Pay basket for *all* of the bills and pay what you can, what is due or overdue, or what is the most critical (such as the utilities). Once the bill is paid, mark the date paid and check number on your portion of the payment stub, and file it with your paid bills, with the most recently paid bill on top of the other papers in the file. You may want to have your financial files in a separate section of your filing system. For example, some of your files for paid bills might be:

Financial — American Express

Financial — J.C. Penney Charge Acct.

Financial — MasterCard

Financial — Mortgage Payments

Financial — Tax Payments

At the end of the year, make sure you pull all of your paid bills, put them into some large envelopes marked with the title and year, and store them (check with your CPA on which bills are tax deductible and on how long you should keep these backup records). Now your financial files are ready to hold the payment records for the upcoming year.

Blueprints. (See Plans.)

Brochures. Brochures are, for the most part, paper dreams. There are those brochures for that cruise that you can't afford and brochures pleading for help for the mountain goats in Timbuktu, mixed in with an abundant assortment of other brochures that, once glanced at, are never looked at again by the average brochure recipient. If you really think you'll have the money and the time for the cruise soon, keep the brochure in a box or file it along with all that other travel stuff (that you probably haven't looked at since you started clipping it). Or you could stuff it in the box or file that features all of the brochures you've hauled home from your various travels over the years. You could do this, but since I think it's silly to keep brochures for any reason, I'd advise you to 1) get rid of all the old brochures by throwing them away, and 2) stop hanging on to the new brochures that come into your life. For example, brochures that want your money or your vote should be read, paid, and/or immediately discarded. Brochures for local services should be perused and the phone number noted on your Rolodex for future reference (throw the brochure away). Travel brochures for potential trips should be kept for a maximum of a few months, then tossed. If you keep them much longer, the prices and other information in them will have changed. Brochures can be bulky and take up a lot of room. It's not worth it; get rid of them!

Budgets. Budgets are put to paper only after great agony and debate. Where the money is coming from, where it should be going, and who gets how much are all questions that are supposed to be answered satisfactorily by the information included in the budget. Nobody likes these things, be it the household budget or the department budget. Nevertheless, they are a fact of life, so if for one reason or another you are obligated to live by one, here are some tips on what to do with them:

1. Get into the act well before the budget is laid down on paper. Pretend that you are an antique dealer; ask for at least 50 percent more money than you want or need. Then negotiate.

2. If you are intimately impacted by the budget, see if you can get your hands on a draft before the final figures are put to paper. That way you can verify that the bean counters got your piece of the pie right. Once it's in its final form, it might as well be written in stone.

3. If yours is a budget for the home, make sure that everybody who is affected by the budget gets to put his or her verbal two cents' worth in as the figures are being compiled. You'll be spared a lot of financial surprises later, and the individual agony may be lessened somewhat as each member of the family adjusts to living within the budget.

4. Once you get the paperwork with the final figures, you can either file it in your Financial section under Budget, or you can tape it on the wall for daily reference and possible dart practice.

Business Cards. People hand out business cards willy-nilly and accept them with about as much abandon. Back in the office, you start to move them from place to place in a half-hearted attempt at figuring out what to actually *do* with them. Whatever you do, do not, I repeat, *do not* put them in those plastic business card holders that hold about a zillion cards altogether. This looks like a good system until you actually need a phone number or name from one of those business cards. Only then do you realize that you have to thumb through all of the cards to get to the one you want because there is no way to efficiently alphabetize the cards as they are put into the plastic sleeves in the first place. You'll be better off if you put the cards with your other phone numbers (keep them in a cigar box or decorative container of some sort) and add them to your Rolodex when you can. Some cards can be trimmed with scissors along the top edge or bottom edge and then stapled directly onto the Rolodex card, saving you the time it would otherwise take to transfer the information. In the end, some cards aren't worth transferring to anything. These are the cards that you accepted when they were offered because you didn't want to be rude. Now that nobody is looking, feel free to throw those cards away. (For more on how to set up a Rolodex, see Phone Numbers.)

Calendars. A calendar for the current year is a must for daily and long-term planning. Depending on your situation, you may want one at work as well as one at home for planning family events. Make your desk calendar one that works well for you (some people prefer small calendars, others work best with larger ones). A family planning calendar at home should probably be posted on the wall and should provide plenty of space under each date for notations such as "Johnny to baseball practice" and "Susie to piano lesson." If you are on the go a lot you'll want your personal calendar to be a portable appointment book that you can check and make notations in while you are out. Resist the urge to have several calendars (which results in duplication or missed information). Also beware of saving old calendars unless you have recorded business appointments or expenses on them, in which case calendars should be saved and filed with your tax records of the corresponding year. Otherwise, throw them away. The bottom line on outdated calendars is *use them or lose them!*

Cards. (See Greeting Cards, Postcards.)

Cartoons. Cartoon clippers like to think that their sense of humor is inherently superior to other people's. Clipped cartoons confirm that idea, and as the clipper files (or piles) said cartoons, lots of smug thoughts go through their funny little heads. What they, and in this case also you, don't stop to consider, though, is that once that cartoon lands in a pile or a file, it's a dead duck. Nobody else will ever see it or know about the cartoon, and if nobody else knows about the cartoon, it's a sure bet they'll never know what a sense of humor you have, you devil, you. So, either post the cartoons in a scrapbook for everyone to enjoy, put them under the glass on your desk (but *not* tacked to the wall or stuck on the refrigerator), or stick them in with your correspondence to give the recipient a chuckle along with your words of wisdom. Whatever you do, don't file them. If it comes to that, you might just as well throw them away. The results are the same, because either way, you'll never see them again.

Catalogues. Once, during a question and answer period of a lecture I was giving, a woman in the audience asked me how long a person should keep catalogues. Responding with my usual intellectual snap, I said, "Well, I dunno, how long do you keep yours?" "Oh," replied the woman, "about four seasons." I never had to say another word in answer to the question, because the audience responded with hysterical laughter that said it all.

I think catalogues serve a terrific purpose. They can be a time-saving alternative to shopping that is as simple as picking up the telephone or filling out an order blank. But keeping catalogues beyond one season or accumulating a year's worth of a particular catalogue is ridiculous. Prices change, and items are not kept in the inventory past a certain date anyway. Some people collect catalogues anyway, hopelessly adding to their mounting piles of paper, magazines, and newspapers. The people who find themselves with uncontrollable catalogue clutter generally fall into one of two categories:

Dreaming Before Deciding—These people dream over catalogues, but when it comes down to the nitty gritty, they can't decide if they want to buy anything or not. So, of course they hold on to the catalogue. Indefinitely.

What to Do: If you're a dreamer who has trouble deciding, try biting the bullet with do or die decisions. When you get a catalogue, put it in your To Read pile and then go through it at your first opportunity, and no, the first opportunity is *not* when you are in the middle of some other distasteful chore. (People just love to stop what they're doing so that they can get to that catalogue that they *have* to look through.) You don't have to look at it right this minute, but when you do peruse it, be prepared to make a decision right then about any purchases that you are going to make—or *Toss the thing in the trash*! A slightly less painful alternative is to cut out the page with the item you are going to buy, pull out the order blank and affix your mailing label from the catalogue, and throw the rest of the catalogue away.

Now as soon as you get the money, attach it to the completed order blank and mail it off.

Catalogue Junkies — Catalogue junkies have no problem whatsoever deciding what to buy — they order something from just about every catalogue that lands in their mailbox. The junkie spends an awful lot of time and money ordering things from catalogues. Then the stuff comes in the mail, and some of it is invariably not the right size or color or whatever, so even more time and money gets spent to send it back. It's a habit, and an expensive one at that.

What to Do: Junkies would do well to try weaning themselves off their habit by not even looking at some of the catalogues that come in the mail. If you get three this week, try tossing one without even looking at it. It's brutal, but you'll survive, and it'll save you money as well.

Whichever type you are, if you've got a catalogue problem, take a look at how many you are receiving each month (check that pile over in the corner if you don't know where to begin). If you're getting more than half a dozen catalogues per quarter, you are definitely past your catalogue limit. Drop a note to some of the more useless catalogue companies and let them know that you can't bear to be faced with so many options and decisions on such a regular basis, so would they kindly remove your name from their mailing list. For those that you do use and like, a nice roomy basket set aside just for catalogues is a good idea. Then, when new catalogues come in, check the basket, and if you have a previous issue of the newly arrived catalogue, throw the old one away and keep only the current one in the basket. This way you'll always be catalogue-current and ready to shop most efficiently by mail.

Charge Accounts. How you handle this paperwork depends on your spending habits. If you have only a couple of charge accounts that you rarely use, a simple file in the Financial section marked Charge Accounts will probably do. But, if you are like most of America and have several credit cards that you use with risky regularity, you will have to set up your files to match your spending habits. Since these are bills that you pay, put them in the Financial section, then title the file by the account, for example, Financial — MasterCard. If you don't have a Financial section, simply label the file by the charge account name, (e.g., MasterCard) and file it alphabetically in your general file. Typical charge account files can include American Express, MasterCard, Visa, department store charges such as Saks Fifth Avenue, Sears, J.C. Penney, auto gas credit cards such as Unocal and Chevron, and special accounts such as Gordon's Grocery and Main Street Stationers.

Thus you may choose to file them all alphabetically by account in the Financial section, or you can integrate them into the general files alphabetically. Still another option is to give a charge account a master heading that places it in a category near other like files. For instance, if you like to keep all of your auto expenses together, you could preface your gas credit card files with Auto, so that now the files would read Auto — Chevron and Auto — Unocal and would be filed in the Auto section of the general files next to other Auto information.

If you have more than one account with the same name, you need to put the account number on your file title to keep the accounts straight. Many people have more than one MasterCard or Visa card, for example, and including the account number on the file and hanging folder tab can help ensure that the proper records are filed in the correct account file.

As you accumulate charge receipts during the month, make sure you save yourself the frustration of searching for those slips of paper at bill-paying time by putting them all in one place during the month. You can drop them into a cigar box or file folder that you keep handy in your desk drawer or on a wall-mounted hot file rack. When it is time to pay the bill, simply compare the slips against the charges on your statement for accuracy. Once the accuracy has been confirmed *you can throw these slips away*. There is no need to keep them, since the information is now on your statement. Make your payment, note the payment amount, the check number, and the date paid on your portion of the statement, and file that portion in the appropriate charge account file.

Once each year, pull these statements from the files, and for those that cannot be deducted for tax purposes, the solution is simple; throw them away. For instance, most of the time you cannot claim a deduction for money spent for clothes at a department store, and assuming you are happy with the merchandise and don't plan to return anything, these statements can be tossed. Charges that can be deducted for business purposes should be segregated during this once-yearly purge. Make a list of these deductible charges and give it to your accountant, or put it in your Tax Back-up file so that when you do your taxes, you will have the list with the expenses. (See Tax Records for more on this subject.) Once you've filed your tax return, keep these statements in 8×10-inch envelopes, marked with the word "Expenses" and the year, and store them in a transfile box in a storage area. Your charge account files in your filing cabinet are now ready to receive all of your charge account paperwork for the coming year.

Finally, you should set up a charge account master file, listing all of your charge accounts, the account number of each one, and the expiration date of each card. Even if you are registered with a service that keeps a record of your accounts, it is helpful to have this list on hand in the event of theft. If any of your cards are stolen, you can pull this list immediately and start notifying the issuer of the card to put a stop on the card at once. Having all of the pertinent information at your fingertips can make this notification process an efficient one.

If all of this charge account paperwork and storage makes you dizzy, you can move to put an end to it by paying off your bills, saving your money, buying less, and using cash to pay for what you do buy. It's a radical concept, and it's probably un-American, but it works.

Charitable Donations. Paperwork that pertains to any donations you make to charities should probably be kept in your Financial section, if you have one, in your files. These donations can be tax deductible, so make sure you pay by check; for back-up, make a note on the bill stub and file it with the date paid (much as you would when paying any other bill). Charities tend to think that your donation will be more likely forthcoming if they send you their plea surrounded by a package of papers that can include heartrending stories, pleas, pictures, all designed to make you give. Throw all of this away. And if you've decided to support a specific charity or two, drop a note to the other charities and ask them to take you off their mailing lists, so that the paper doesn't come into your house or office in the first place. If, on the other hand, you are actively involved in several charities, you may want to keep the paperwork straight by setting up a file for each major charity, either in your financial files or in the general file system or both. If, for example, you are a major donor to your museum, you will want a file set up in the Financial section, and you may also want to set up a file in the general section to house the information that you will regularly receive about improvements to the museum, exhibitions, and other related material. (For information on how to keep paperwork for meetings, such as Board of Directors meetings you may be attending, see Meeting Records.)

Sample titles of your charitable files could be:

Financial—Charitable Donations (Filed in Financial files). You only need this one file for all of your donations unless you are a major donor at one or more charities.

Financial—Charitable Donations (Followed by name of charity) (filed in Financial files). This file, with the specific name of a single charity, should be opened for any charity with which you maintain an active and substantial financial relationship.

Charity. (Followed by name of charity) (filed in General files). However you do your giving, remember that when it comes to charity's paperwork, it is far better to give than to receive, so feel free to write out the checks and toss unnecessary paperwork that you have received at the same time.

Children's Papers. Children's papers include their medical and school records, important documents such as their birth certificate, and the schoolwork and artwork that they drag home by the truckload. Your files should only have important papers such as their medical records, birth certificate, and any other important documents. Give each child his or her own file in the appropriate section of the system. For example:

Medical – Shari   Documents – Shari

Medical – Tommy   Documents – Tommy

The medical files can contain immunization records as well as any other treatment and diagnosis records of each child. The Documents files could hold the birth certificate and any other important document the child might have, such as a passport. *Important* is a key word, because it can be easy for a loving mother to think that everything the little darling brings home is important, such as that test that Shari got an A+ on last year. This is nice, this is even wonderful for mother and little Shari, but it is not an important document that should be choking up mother's files. If your children go to private school, you might have to add another file for each child for the school year. This file will hold all of the instructions you will receive on uniforms, schedules, car pools, and roster that you will get throughout the year. Although much of this information is important, if you really read it when it comes in, and it's not complicated information, you can probably throw it away. If you think you'll forget something, or you have some responsibility to keep track of (such as with a car pool schedule, for example), then file it. Otherwise toss it.

If you're still wondering what to do with that A+ test paper, your answer is to purchase a rolling basket system (one for each child). These carts can be used to hold all manner of things, but one of the best adaptations for use is to set it up for the children's school papers and artwork. You can eliminate the problem of what to do with the school papers forever with this cart. Simply turn the top of the cart into a filing cart by installing hanging files on rails (which can be purchased with the cart). Label the hanging files Awards, Reading, Spelling, Writing, and so on. Inside each hanging file, place a manila filing folder with the same label (just as you would in your own filing cabinet). Now your children can proudly show you their daily schoolwork, and after you have oohed and aahed over it, they can just as proudly file it in their own "filing cabinet." This system teaches and creates organization at the same time.

Two or three oversized baskets can be installed under the hanging file portion of the rolling cart to provide the perfect storage solution for school supplies and artwork that the children bring home—from those macaroni marvels to the special holiday works of art that are made with love and tons of talent. Carry on as much as you want when the art comes into the house, and then lay it lovingly to rest in the rolling cart.

At the end of the school year, sort through the manila file folders, selecting the best papers and artwork. Then put them in a transfile box, mark the box with your child's age and the year, and store the box as mementos. You can either remove the papers from the manila file folders and store them flat in the transfile box (which means you can reuse the manila folders for next year), or you can store the papers in the box still in the manila folders (in this case you would have to make up new manila file folders to place in the already labeled hanging file folders for next year).

Be careful not to keep every scrap of paper that your children bring home. If you do, you'll need to rent a warehouse to store it all. Move only the best schoolwork and pieces of art into your yearly storage box and, when nobody is looking, throw the rest away.

This one cart should take your child through high school, serving as a school records and art and supply center, and can be rolled to the homework area as needed. When the little darling finally does leave the nest, you can use the cart yourself for clothes, projects, linens, or hobby or stationery supplies.

Client Records. Client files are best kept alphabetically, under the client's last name. If you want to keep all of the clients together, simply start a Client subsection in your general files. If you do this you might have these files:

Client—John Babcock

Client—Wendy Murphy

Client—James Wilson

If your business is client-based, you may need to assign a drawer or even a bank of files to your client files. Make sure you put Client on your manila folder so that the file goes back to the right drawer or bank of cabinets.

If your client files generate a lot of diversified activity, you might want to break the files down a bit more, particularly for your larger clients. For example, you might have:

Client—John Babcock—Correspondence

Client—John Babcock—Invoices

Client—John Babcock—Orders

For client files that show minimal activity, you might want some general files such as:

Clients—Miscellaneous Invoices

Clients—Miscellaneous Orders

or vice versa:

Clients—Invoices, Miscellaneous

Clients—Orders, Miscellaneous

Remember to base your decision on how you will remember it. For example, will you remember it as *miscellaneous* information, or will you remember it as *invoices* first, before you think of miscellaneous?

How you set up your client files depends entirely on how you think of them and on how much paperwork activity each client generates. Your client files should be looked at once each year, and if there has been no activity on a client's account in over a year, you might want to give the file to someone who will try to bring the client back to life with a reorder, or you might want to put the file into storage. You can also throw the file out altogether if you would not be impacted legally by such a move. After all, after about a year and half, the chances are that your prices and methods of doing business will have changed enough to make the information in the file out of date (legal and medical files excepted, of course). You may want to consider transferring important information to a card or computer system and trashing the rest of the old paperwork on these "dead" clients. However you decide to do it, remember that an inactive client is not bringing you money; indeed the maintenance and storage of their file is costing you money in labor and square footage. You can focus more effectively on your current clients if their files are not crowded to the point of obscurity in the filing cabinets by the files of inactive or dead clients. So move the dying to intensive care, bury the dead, and get on with the business of serving the clients that keep your business going—the live ones!

Clippings. (See Mementos, Cartoons, Articles.)

College Papers. Dusty college papers always make me think of school, and school makes me think of tests. If you've read my other books, you've heard this before, and maybe you've even taken my "college papers quiz" before. If so, and if you are reading this section again, obviously the other books didn't help you with this paper problem. So for the uninitiated, and for those who *still* have boxes of college papers, in spite of what they've heard me say before, here's my college papers test to help you really get in the spirit of things:

1. *How* many years have you been holding on to those papers?
   ☐ 2 or less ☐ 2-5 years ☐ 5-10 years ☐ more than 10 years

2. *Why* are you keeping them? (Check all that apply):
   ☐ I'm so brilliant, I got terrific grades, and those papers are a testament to my unparalleled intelligence.
   ☐ I might need them for reference someday.
   ☐ My English Lit papers remind me that I was voted Class Clown for three years in a row.

3. *Where* are these papers stored, and how much square footage do they occupy?

4. Now (here's a little math for you) multiply the square footage by the cost of that space and write in the total dollar amount below:

5. Have the bugs found your precious papers yet? (Hint: If they haven't, it's only a matter of time until they do.)

Scoring:

There is no scoring system for this quiz. There is almost no way to pass this particular test, since there is no earthly reason that I can think of to save college papers (and/or textbooks). If you are convinced that you'll need them for reference, I'd like to remind you that times change, and reference materials become outdated practically every other minute. Libraries can provide all of the reference you will ever need, and in all likelihood, we're talking about a trip to the library once every five or six years (if that), which is a much more sensible approach to the issue of "reference." You won't need these papers someday. They are a pathetic excuse for memorabilia (if you're determined to keep junk and call it memorabilia, you can do better than this), and they are taking up too much space and drawing bugs in the process (bugs love piles of papers; they turn them into bug highrises and condos). There's only one thing to do with these papers. Let go of the past by letting go of your college papers. Courage will help you move once and for all into the present.

Contracts. Contracts, regardless of how careful you are when you negotiate them, can come back to haunt you. So make sure you make it easy to get your hands on any contracts you may have (in the event of a dispute). File them in a Contracts file or files. But before you sign and file *any* contract, take your time and try to cut the best deal you can.

Corporate Records. Corporate records, including the corporate minutes, articles of incorporation, and corporate seal, should be kept in good order in a safe place, preferably in a fireproof safe or filing cabinet. The minutes can be organized in a binder chronologically and should always be kept up to date—a sharp tsk tsk to those of you who haven't paid attention to officially updating those records as required by law. Check with your accountant and/or your attorney regarding how often these documents need to be reviewed and/or updated. Also, have these professionals advise you whether new paperwork that is generated might best be considered a part of the corporate records and therefore be stored with the other corporate documents.

Correspondence. It is not, contrary to popular belief, necessary to keep *all* correspondence. Cover letters, stupid letters, and letters asking for money for causes that you don't believe in can be instantly tossed. Letters with hopelessly out-of-date information can also be given the heave-ho. Old love letters can be fun to keep, but you don't need to keep a trunkful—a shoebox will definitely do (for more on this, see Love Letters). Keep the correspondence that needs to be kept for sentimental, legal, or financial purposes by category in files, boxes, or storage files. A regular and ruthless culling of letters as they are opened can keep these papers under considerable control in the long run.

Having said all of that, let's take a closer look at your correspondence. Correspondence generally falls into two areas, business and personal. You might want to start, therefore, with two files:

Correspondence—Business

Correspondence—Personal

These correspondence categories can be broken down further, depending on the volume of correspondence that you send and/or receive. If you correspond with great regularity with certain people, you might need to give them their own correspondence file. For example:

Correspondence — XYZ Vending Company

Correspondence — Aunt Thelma

The correspondence that you receive, along with the copy of your responses should all be placed in the file chronologically, with the most recent correspondence on top. A trick to help you limit the volume of paperwork is to type or write your correspondence response and execute the carbon on the *back* of the letter you are responding to. For example, XYZ Vending Co. writes to you about a problem. You need to write a letter back to address their problem. Take their letter, turn it over, put a piece of carbon on top of it, cover that with a piece of stationery, and type your response directly onto the back of their original letter to you.

Be aware, as you set up your correspondence files, of the pitfalls of setting up a Correspondence — Miscellaneous file. This always turns into a dumping ground. In fact, all correspondence files have a tendency to turn into dumping grounds, with people automatically dumping all correspondence into the file without any thought as to the value of keeping the letter in the first place. Cover letters usually do *not* need to be kept. After all, why would you keep a letter with three sentences in it that says, essentially, "Here is the material that you want"? You'll be putting the material in the file (with the date of the receipt of the correspondence stamped on it), so why do you need the letter as well? Think about the letters that you file *before* you file them, and you'll find yourself throwing some of them away before they even have a chance to land in those files. (If you're worried about losing their address, put it on your Rolodex.)

Your correspondence files should be cleaned out at least once each year, and preferably more often; unless the letters have legal or financial significance, or unless they pertain to ongoing issues, much of what is in these correspondence files can be tossed on a fairly regular basis. It can be especially difficult to purge personal correspondence files, since often there is a sentimental value attached to those letters. Nevertheless, a careful culling can result in the elimination of some of the letters, and if you simply can't get rid of the rest, move them out of the filing cabinet and into a memorabilia box or album of some kind that can then be stored on a bookshelf, in a cabinet, or a closet.

Decorating Ideas. If you're thinking about redecorating, you'll want to set up a file to hold clippings showing decorating schemes that you favor. Once you actually start renovating or redecorating, you can break these files down by function, since a great deal of paperwork can be generated to accompany the aggravation that goes along with the do-over of any room or house. You may want to put all of these files under the heading of House as well since, ultimately, some of what you do may be tax deductible or have some relevance to the resale value of your house should you decide to sell. For example, let's say you are going to renovate the kitchen and the master bedroom and bath. Once the project has moved out of the idea stage and into the action stage, you could set up the following files for the paperwork that will be generated:

House — Renovation — Fabric and Furniture Purchases

House — Renovation — Kitchen

House — Renovation — Master Bedroom

House — Renovation — Master Bath

You may even want to set up one file for contracts, since you may be doing business with different people (although it is certainly best to deal with as few people as possible). This file could be titled House Renovation — Contracts.

Assuming you get from the dreaming/decorating idea stage to the doing stage, and assuming you accomplish your renovation without having to resort to legal action against any of the people who do the work for you, *and* assuming the whole process doesn't give you a nervous breakdown, you can go through the files and weed out any material that is no longer appropriate. Papers with ideas that you decided against, or even ideas that you did use, can be tossed. Dozens of swatches can also be ditched, since you have settled on the fabric and it is on the wall or at the windows now. Keep only cost and contract information, and keep it with your other House documents (see House Records for more on this). These files should be kept in the current general file for one year after the work is done, against the very likely event that something should go wrong and you have to summon the contractor or decorator back to fix the problem. After resting about a year in your current files, these files can be moved to a storage area or even tossed if your improvements are determined to be nondeductible, or if the actual costs of the improvements have no direct bearing on the resale value of your home.

Dental. Dental records and bills should be filed in the Medical section of your file. (For more on this, see Medical.)

Disaster Recovery Plan. (See pages 46-49.)

Entertainment and Party Planning. If you entertain regularly, you will want to set up files to keep track of certain things so that you can refer back to those files for information as needed. For example, you may want to keep a file with information on caterers and their available menus and prices, and you might keep a file on the different types of entertainment available for hire. If you are planning a very special, large party, you might also want to set up a file for that particular event to keep track of all of the details, to hold the guest list and so on, which can later be added to your mementos. And if you give lots of parties with themes, you may want to maintain an idea file. If you are the hostess with the mostest, you can even put the guest list on your computer with appropriate notations next to each name. You could include each guest's preferences as well as information about which events you had invited them to (and which ones you had not). Below are some typical Entertaining files:

Entertaining – Caterers

Entertaining – Entertainment

Entertaining – Guest Lists

Entertaining – Harry's Fiftieth, 1990

Entertaining – Ideas

Entertaining – Sid's Bar Mitzvah, 1990

(These are examples of 'special' events.)

For the person who entertains regularly, many of these files are important resource files that are referred to frequently. From time to time, when you have the file out, take just a moment to toss outdated information so that the file doesn't become too cluttered and therefore more difficult to use. The special events files should be moved to a memorabilia area (box or album) after any pertinent information, such as the guest list, is photocopied and placed into the other resource files.

Expense Reports. If a significant amount of your time at work is spent traveling to see clients or wining and dining them, then you have the added paper burden of expense reports in your life. You don't need this aggravation, but there it is. If you want to recover the money that you spent you have to fill these reports out, and furthermore, you had better double-check your math and include all of the receipts with those reports. It's a known fact that the bean counters in accounting are lobbying for the death penalty for people who screw up their expense reports. You know that, of course, but it still always seems much easier said than done, what with your busy schedule, so this is one paper problem that is allowed to go unattended until it becomes a paper monster. Finally you scoop up all of the receipts, try to remember what amount of money was paid of what, where, and who, and do your level best to get it all in order so it can be sent to accounting. Some people cheat a little, of course, and this just makes dealing with the paper documentation all the more difficult. Regardless of your methods, invariably the stuff gets organized (sort of) and sent to accounting about three weeks *after* you need the money to pay your own charge account bills (where those company-related charges are now appearing). Accounting has no patience whatsoever with you, because they know you always do this — half the time your report is wrong or questionable — and they don't care *when* you want the money, you'll get it in the next pay-out cycle, whenever that may be.

Your financial life can be made easier by following a few guidelines. First, always carry an envelope in your inside pocket, handbag, or briefcase. As soon as you get a receipt, mark the date and client name or reason for the expense on the receipt and put it into the envelope. At the end of the day, quickly add up the receipts inside the envelope by category (e.g., meals, travel, etc.). Put this recap along with the total for the day on the front of the envelope and put another empty envelope in your pocket or bag. Once each week simply gather up the envelopes, add up the total for each category, and transfer the information to your expense report. If you have a secretary, he or she won't have any more "I can't understand this mess" excuses, and you can give it to that person to transfer the information. Have him or her or someone else photocopy the whole mess (the report plus the receipts in the envelopes) and send the original receipts — still in the envelopes is fine — on to accounting. You keep the copies in an active file in your desk. When you are paid for that report, mark it Paid, and move it out of your desk and into the filing cabinet.

If you need the figures from these reports at tax time, pull the file and give your accountant the figures. Then if your accountant gives you permission, throw those paper monsters away. Otherwise, put them in storage with your other paper monsters — your tax records.

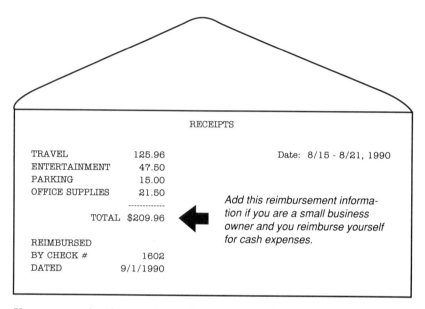

Keep your receipts in a business-sized envelope when you travel, and for easy reimbursement and recordkeeping purposes simply provide a recap of the receipts on the front of the envelope.

JBL Graphics, Montrose, California

Expenses. (See also Bills, Receipts.) You may choose to add the word "Expenses" to the files in your Financial section that relate to the expenses that you incur and subsequently pay throughout the year. If you have only a few files, you can establish some very broad file categories such as:

Expenses — Business

Expenses — House

Expenses — Personal

Most people, however, have too many expenses to handle their files in this manner. Because of the quantity of expenses that can be incurred on a monthly and quarterly basis, it is best to establish different files for these regular expenses. This method keeps the paperwork neatly categorized and organized, and if there is a problem with any one creditor or supplier, the information that you need to pull about that account is all in one file, with no other papers to get in your way. You may want to file your expenses under the title of the expense, such as Telephone or Rent, or you may want to put it in the Financial drawer, with a subcategory of Expenses, thus locating all of the expenses under *E* with the creditor then falling in line alphabetically. Unless you have an abundance of other nonexpense-related files in the Financial drawer, I recommend the simpler method of listing only the expense title and filing it alphabetically (Telephone, for instance, would fall under *T* in the Financial drawer). So you could choose to file your expenses in either of these two ways:

Financial — Expenses — Postage	or	Financial — Postage
Financial — Expenses — Rent	or	Financial — Rent
Financial — Expenses — Telephone	or	Financial — Telephone
Financial — Expenses — Utilities	or	Financial — Utilities

Although it is tempting to adopt a careless attitude about the paperwork that represents your expenses (otherwise known as bills), it is probably best if you do *not* throw the paid bill stubs away or do as so many people tend to do — stuff all of the paid stubs into one humongous manila envelope or cigar box. This stuffing method is fine only if you never have a problem with anybody, and only if your checks and canceled checks are in perfectly organized order. Even then, I think it is much more time-consuming to sift through canceled checks to determine whether or not a bill was paid than it is to simply pull a single file and spend just a few seconds to review your payment record, which is marked and filed in chronological order within that file.

At the end of the year, you can pull these expense records and then, after you have made any applicable notations and calculations where specific expenses might be considered tax deductible, file these records in a large manila envelope and store them in the inactive filing cabinet or storage box. Fasten each category of bills together with a paper clip, put them neatly in the envelope, and mark the front of the envelope with Expenses and the year. Throw away all of the expense records that are not tax deductible. Your Expense files are now empty and ready to receive the paid bill stubs and other expense records that you will accumulate over the next taxable, expensive year.

Family Records. (See also Children's Papers, Medical Records, Important Documents, and The Master File.) Family records should be incorporated alphabetically into the current general filing system or, in the case of financial matters, into the financial section. For certain records, you will want to indicate the individual family member's name, and then it is a judgment call as to whether you want that person's name first or the category first. For example, let's say you have two children, Freddy and John:

Medical — Freddy		Freddy — Medical
Medical — John		John — Medical
	or	
School Records — Freddy		Freddy — School Records
School Records — John		John — School Records

If you opt to put the family member's name first, the benefit is that all of that person's files would be located in the same place in the drawer, that is, all of John's files would be together under *J* and all of Freddy's records would be together under *F*. The disadvantage is that you may be including files and records that are tax related (such as medical receipts that may be deductible) in the general files, when they really should be in the Financial section of your files. In the long run, I do recommend the topic first, then the name. Thus, all of the School records would be under *S* and all of the family's Medical records would be under *M*, with each family member having a file of his or her own for each category.

Other documents, such as birth certificates and the like, can be in an Important Document file or in a safety deposit box. (For more information on which important documents to keep and where to keep them, along with how to set up a Master file, see The Master File on pages 45-46 and the Disaster Recovery Plan on pages 46-49.)

If you are developing a family history or family tree, you can set up files, but a more comprehensive approach is to set up a three-ring binder with dividers. You can divide the book by family members, for example, one section for Great Grandfather on Mother's side, and one section for Great Grandfather on Father's side, and on down the line. Then as you accumulate information on any one person, you can put it into that section. You can also try to set your binder up in years or generations, marking off a section for every twenty-five or thirty years or so, and you can put information in those sections chronologically, as you accumulate it. If you receive newspaper clippings or letters that you don't want to punch holes into, you can use plastice sheet protectors from the stationery store. These have holes punched into them already and a clear pocket that you can slip the clipping or letter into so that you can still keep it in the binder. Don't forget to add a special section for names and addresses as well as one for special dates (births, marriages, etc.). When you have finished your research, you will have a family history "book" assembled for anyone who wants to look at it for years to come. You can add to it as the years go by, and in generations to come, it can serve as a complete resource file for those who might want to carry on the tradition of maintaining the family historical records.

Financial Statements. File these in the Financial drawer under Financial—Statements. Make sure the most current statement is on top, and if you need to have these updated regularly, you may even want to mark the year on each folder. As soon as last year's statements have been updated and replaced more than once or twice, you can move the old statements to your archival files where you can store them alongside other financial and tax-related matters.

Forms. If you use a lot of different forms, chances are fair to good that you have them scattered all over the place, with some in and on your desk, some on top of the filing cabinet, and some inside; you may even have batches of them stacked here and there on the bookcase or floor. The first step when it comes to forms is to go through the forms and ask yourself if you *really* use it. If it is outdated, toss it immediately. If you still have dozens of forms that you need to have on hand, you can organize them into file folders that can be dropped into hanging folders either in your desk drawer, in a rolling cart, or in a two-drawer filing cabinet placed right next to your desk. This puts the forms at your fingertips—you won't even have to get out of your chair. And by putting forms into the files (as opposed to your previous piles), you can grab the one you want when you want it. (Title these forms alphabetically, e.g., Forms—Applications, or Forms—Expense Reimbursement.)

If you only have a few forms that you use from time to time, you won't need an entire drawer or cart, of course. You can still put them in your desk file drawer, or you can purchase a stationery divider that lays flat in one of your regular desk drawers; you can organize and keep your forms separate in this divided tray. Or you can hang a divided hot file over your desk with one type of form in each of three or four slots. All of these methods keep the forms within your immediate reach and at the same time prevent them from getting mixed up in a hopeless pile that requires time-wasting digging to locate what you need when you need it. Whenever any form is declared obsolete or is replaced by a new version, destroy the old forms at once. They only take up precious space, and having them around invites everybody to accidentally use an old form that is no longer acceptable.

Frequent Flyer Records. (See Travel.)

Greeting Cards. People tend to have two types of greeting cards on hand—the ones they have received and the new ones they plan to send out (someday). Greeting cards are somehow intertwined with guilt and good intentions, and are further complicated by one's sensibilities, artistic and otherwise. The guilt works like this: Lots of people send you greeting cards, and it was such a nice gesture, you'd actually feel *bad* if you got rid of them. Plus the card is an obvious reminder of what a special person you are. Then too, you feel a little guilty because now you owe them a card. Which, as it happens, you're going to send as soon as you get the chance to sit down and make out an envelope. You may have to wait until you get to the store to purchase the card that you now need to send to this wonderful, thoughtful person who has just now sent you a card. Or maybe you have to wait until you get to the post office. In the meantime, you don't throw that greeting card away. This guilt circle never quits, and most of the time, more cards come in than go out, and even if you get around to sending a card yourself, you won't throw their card out because 1) it was so nice of them to think of you, 2) the message on the card is terribly touching and/ or funny, or 3) the photo or artwork on the card is fabulous. So you stuff these cards into your filing cabinet and in piles in the back of drawers.

Greeting card addicts—that is, people who can't pass a card shop without buying at least a dozen *fabulous* cards to send out *someday*—have an even greater problem. First of all, there are all the cards that they've received. Then there are the dozens and dozens of greeting cards that they've purchased. (Card addicts always purchase ten times more than they'll ever send out.) If this sounds like you, begin by resolving to respond to greeting cards that you receive *only if it is really necessary and called for*, and if it is called for, to send your card out *within one week* of receipt of their card. If you have a healthy stock of greeting cards on hand, resist the urge to buy any more until you have made a substantial dent in your current supply. Keep only the most special cards that arrive in the mail and throw the rest away. Put those cards in a memorabilia box or album so that you can reminisce over them if you like; your files will not be choked up with these paper cards that prove how wonderful you really are.

If you've collected Christmas cards that have been sent to you, you can now cheerfully send them on to the St. Jude's Ranch for Children, a home for abused and unwanted children. The children at the school use the cards to make new holiday cards by cutting the pictures off the used ones and gluing the pictures onto new backing. The school sells the final product and uses the funds to help with their operating costs. Send your used *Christmas cards only* to: St. Jude's Ranch for Children, Box 985, Boulder City NV 89005.

Finally, so that your supply of fresh cards doesn't choke up important paper storage space, you might consider putting them in a basket with a handle on it, and never buy more than what fits in the basket. Make sure your supply features some generic cards as well as some of the basics — Happy Birthday, Happy Anniversary, and Thank You. By keeping the basics at hand, you'll be able to resist the temptation and avoid the time it takes to run out and get a specific card for an immediate need. Keep some postage and a good pen in the basket, and you can carry the basket to your easy chair, your bedside, or to the table where you have your afternoon break. The next time you light in any one of these areas, take a minute, reach down, grab a card, and send it out!

Health Information. This file would include any articles or other information on health-related issues that might affect you now or in the future. For example, if you are starting to develop arthritis, you might be accumulating information that you come across on the topic for your reference now and possibly into the future if the arthritis gets worse. Put the file in your general files under Health Information. Make sure, however, that you don't mix medical records, diagnosis information, or bills in this file (those should go in your Medical file). This is only a resource or general information file, nothing more. Clean this out at least once a year, since you will no doubt find that health issues and your interest in them change over time, depending on your health, age, and lifestyle.

House Records. Records that apply directly to the house itself can include mortgage and purchase documents, renovation or improvement paperwork, and repair records. Since repairs generally don't have the same application in taxable or resale terms that improvements do, you will want to separate these records. Here are some potential House files that you might want to set up and install in your general filing system:

House — Improvements

House — Mortgage and Purchase Documents

House — Repairs

All other household accounts should be filed under the appropriate account name. For example, if you receive regular service from a gardener, you'll need a gardener file. Utilities should be under Utilities, and if you keep receipts for new furniture purchases (although I don't know why you would, unless there is a warranty, or it's for your office and your accountant tells you it's tax deductible), you might want a file titled simply Furniture. Thin these files out every year by moving the previous year's paperwork to storage. Some of the papers can be tossed, but in all cases, of course, you must keep your purchase documents. In fact, generally these, along with any paperwork connected with the sale or disposition of your house, must also be kept well after the transition has been made. Consult the IRS or your accountant for more detailed retention schedule information on this asset.

Important Documents. This file can hold the oddball pieces of paper that are important documents. These can be any documents that you choose not to store in a safety deposit box but don't want to set up an entire file for because there is only one piece of paper. Examples are birth certificates, marriage licenses, military discharge papers, and passports. Make sure you let key people and/or family members know about this file in the event of an emergency, or in case they need to retrieve one of the documents for their own personal reasons. This file is really only good if you find yourself with just a few important documents. If your important paperwork is extensive and includes, for example, important insurance policies, birth certificates, and much more, refer back to pages 45-49 for information on a Master file and a Disaster Recovery Plan.

Insurance. Insurance documents, policies, and payment records should be kept in your general or Financial files under the Insurance subcategory and then further broken down by type of insurance. For example, you may need these insurance files:

Financial—Insurance—Auto

Financial—Insurance—Health

Financial—Insurance—House

Financial—Insurance—Life

It is more efficient to group the insurance files together under *I* than to distribute them separately based on the category (putting house insurance under *H* for house, for instance). You may want to keep the actual policies in a safety deposit box, but make sure a designated heir or executor has access to the box in the event of your death. And be sure to list important policy information in your Master file (see pages 45-46).

Another way to store insurance files—particularly if you don't generate or accumulate too much paperwork—is to store the paperwork in one specially divided file folder, using *Insurance* as the main category or subject and noting on each divider in the folder the type of insurance paperwork filed behind the divider. These special file folders are extra sturdy and can have as many as eight divided compartments. Often referred to as classification folders, they can be used, for instance, to classify your insurance papers and policies under Insurance – Auto; Insurance – Health; Insurance – House; and Insurance – Life. Whenever you pull the file, you have *all* of your insurance paperwork organized immediately at hand. You do still want to place this potentially larger file folder inside a hanging file folder, which in this case would be titled, simply, Insurance. If your Insurance file seems too fat for the hanging file, you can use a box-bottom hanging file or return to using a separate file for each type of insurance paperwork.

Filing all insurance paperwork logically is vital, particularly when one considers the legal and/or financial ramifications of a misplaced claim or a lapsed policy. To avoid nasty surprises about insurance issues, organize the paperwork within the file specifically and chronologically for easy reference and retrieval. Set up a separate file for each type of insurance and keep claims and claim forms in a separate file titled Insurance – Claims.

Setting up Claims Files. While it's relatively simple to keep track of insurance payments, insurance claims paperwork is all too often mired in confusion that is only made worse when the records are not organized properly in your files. If you have a large claim that generates an abundance of paperwork, you may want to set up a file for that claim only, e.g., Insurance – Claim – Garage Fire. Other claim files can be more general in nature. For example, medical claims generally are filed throughout the year for minor and major visits to the doctors. Claims are filed even if you have a deductible, and the paperwork that is returned to you confirming your claim can be used to keep track of how far along you are in satisfying the deductible. Once the deductible is met, you or your doctor can then be reimbursed by your insurance company. Whether you are dealing with Medicare or with a private insurance firm, it pays to keep careful tabs on your claims paperwork so that you know exactly who owes whom what and when at all times.

To keep your claims straight, make a copy of any bills you submit along with your claim form. File these bills with a copy of your claim on the right side of your claims file (clamp it down with a bracket). When the confirmation of each claim is returned to you (the confirmation should show what the insurance company is paying or how much has been applied to your deductible) file this inside the claims folder on the left side of the file folder. Find the copy of the claim that is being confirmed (filed on the right side of the folder) and make a note at the top indicating the date of the confirmation notice and how much of the bill (if any) was paid by the insurance company. It can also be helpful to note who received the payment — you or the professional who billed you. Thus, the paperwork on the left will all directly relate in some manner to the paperwork on the right, which is organized so that you can see what has not been paid by the insurer or spot a mispayment the minute it comes in the mail.

Policies and Payments. Unless you store them in a safety deposit box, all policies and the accompanying paperwork (amendments, applications, etc.) should be filed chronologically on the right side of the folder, with payment documentation placed chronologically inside the folder on the left side of the file (this is a case where clamping the papers down with brackets is also essential).

One more insurance tip: If you want to stay on top of the payments, you can note when the bills will arrive on your calendar for six to twelve months in advance, and you'll be prepared in advance for upcoming payments. For instance, your auto insurance may be payable twice yearly, and your health insurance payable quarterly. By making a note on your calendar on the appropriate months, you will know when to expect and budget for all of your insurance payments. Once the bill actually arrives, put it immediately into your To Pay basket and make sure that when you review the bills in the basket (which should be done at least twice a month) you pay the insurance bill promptly so that it doesn't lapse on you.

Inventory Records. In this day and age, most people have inventory records computerized, where — they tell me — a push of a button or two records and charts everything you ever wanted to know about every single widget you may or may not have in your warehouse. If you are terribly low tech or without a computer, you can make do with a card system that can be kept in a card tray or on a large Rolodex. This quickly becomes labor intensive, of course; so, regardless of your anticomputer sentiments, the truth is that you probably can't ignore it any longer. Get a computer.

If you're not in the widget business, you may still have an inventory to consider. You may want to inventory personal effects, jewelry, furnishings, or art and antiques. Particularly where there are items of value concerned, you might want to photograph the item and draw up a description of the article to go along with it. You can purchase plastic sheet protectors with pockets that can accommodate photos or snapshots. Place a piece of three-hole punched paper opposite the photo describing the item in the photo, and keep these documents in a binder in a safe place (preferably in a fire-proof cabinet or safety deposit box). You may want to go a step further and assign a number to each item, with a corresponding number on the description. This can be especially helpful if you are considering selling or giving any part of the inventory away; you can refer to any piece by number, which can then be referenced for a more complete description. You'll save yourself the time spent repeatedly describing the item(s) in legal documentation.

Keep your inventory as long as you have the items described in the inventory. When something is sold, unless there are tax, divorce, or other legal implications, there is no need to keep either the photo or description. Remember, too, when something new is added to your personal effects or collections to enter a new photo, number, and description into your inventory book.

Investment Records. These records can cover a wide range of investments, from stocks and bonds to mutual funds and real estate. Some people like to preface all of their investment files with the word "Investment," and you might want to do this as well. For example, you might have these files:

Financial — Investments — Property — Arizona

Financial — Investments — Property — Florida

Financial — Investments — Property — Merrill Lynch

Financial — Investments — Property — Taylor Partnership

By grouping all of these files in your Financial section under *I* you can go right to *all* of your investments (which are located in the *I* section). For people who engage in a lot of financial activity, however, this can sometimes become burdensome. It's fine if you do all of your filing yourself, but if you have someone else filing for you, they might not understand your financial dealings as well as you do and therefore might not be able to determine which papers have to do with your "investments." If this is the case, a simpler system is to simply group your records alphabetically and as simply as possible. For instance:

Financial — Arizona Property

Financial — Florida Property

Financial — Merrill Lynch

Financial — Taylor Partnership

I always vote for the simplest title to ensure easy recall and therefore easy retrieval, and to make it as straightforward as possible for the person doing the filing.

Check with your accountant regarding the length of time that you are required to keep these records (you can look forward to hanging on to these for a while, I'm sure). But do move the records to storage unless they are relatively current (within the last year or two). Also, go through these files periodically; while you have to keep a great deal of the paperwork, you can often get rid of some of it (duplicates, cover letters, and confirmation slips on stocks already sold, for instance). Investments are important. Treat the paperwork that accompanies them with care, and you'll find that some of your most important affairs are always in order.

Invoices. Invoices should be treated as bills, paid bills, or expenses. For more information on this see *Bills* or *Expenses*.

Junk Mail. Junk mail is a blanket term used to describe everything from charity pleas, political protest announcements, and catalogues to unsolicited stickers and stamps (which are usually coupled with charity pleas). People complain about junk mail, but they can get awfully attached to it, even when they are complaining. I think junk mail should be thrown away, period. And, not only that, I think you should send a form letter to the people who send you the junk mail and tell them that you are moving and you won't pay the forwarding charges, so please take your name off the list. Don't forget to include the label from the junk mail, since their computers have a very meaningful relationship with those labels.

In the end, most junk mail does not contribute to the daily quality of one's life whatsoever. People can make charitable contributions, vote, and purchase consumer goods completely on their own — without the relentless prodding that arrives via the junk mail. Knowing that, I don't know why more people don't put a trash can right next to the mailbox so that they can drop the junk mail into the can before it ever goes into the house or office. No need to open it, just dump it. Why do you think they call it junk mail?

Legal Documents. Legal documents pertaining to a lawsuit or legal inquiry of any kind should be filed as concisely as possible. This can sometimes be difficult, since a lot of paperwork that accompanies legal action can be somewhat confounding to the layperson. Begin by assigning a case name to the documents. You can then file it under the case name, or you can begin by setting aside a Legal section in the files (a good idea if you anticipate a great deal of paperwork before the case is resolved). Keeping things in chronological order can be important legally, so as you generate new files, you may want to note dates on the manila folder — particularly if the case stretches over several years' time. Beyond that, you can set up files according to the paperwork that is in the file. If you're stumped as to what the paperwork actually is, you can usually find a title on the top page of any set of documents you receive. For example:

Legal — Culp vs. Culp — Affidavits (Date)

Legal — Culp vs. Culp — Deposition (Date)

Legal — Culp vs. Culp — Discovery (Date)

Legal — Culp vs. Culp — Pleadings (Date)

You can file these alphabetically, or — since, with a little bit of luck, legal events occur in a sequence leading to trial — you may just want to file them in separate files, with the most recent action in a file in the front. Then, of course, there is the matter of the legal bills for this case. Ouch. Put that under:

Legal — Culp vs. Culp — Bills (Mr. Lawyer)

Are you sure you want to go through with this case?

Logs. Logs are useful for keeping track of certain information, such as mail received and how it was routed, or to record visitors who check in at the reception desk. Time and phone logs can keep track of how you spend your time and who made what phone calls, and mileage logs can be used to keep the required information to claim miles traveled as a deduction at tax time. If you routinely use logs for these or any other reasons, the best way to keep them organized is to keep them in a binder of some kind. You can use a large three-ring binder, or you can use a smaller appointment book-sized binder to hold your logs. When the binder becomes full, simply remove some of the logs and store them in other binders on a shelf, leaving the log that you use on a daily basis with only current records. Periodically, you can move these binders to storage or throw some of the dated information away altogether, particularly if there is no legal or financial reason to hang onto them. (You may want to check with your CPA or the IRS to see what, if any, special-record keeping requirements may apply to your particular situation.)

Love Letters. (See also Correspondence, Mementos.) Most people think love letters should be tossed as soon as you enter into a marriage or a long-term, live-in relationship. Not me. I think old love letters serve a very important purpose; they make you feel young and special and can quite often serve as a quick pick-me-up on an otherwise dreadful day. Although I do think that they can be thinned out as the years wear on, a selection of the very best deserve to go down in history with you. Besides thinning them out (volumes of letters can be egotistically excessive, after all), the important thing to do is to find an appropriate hiding place for the few you decide to keep around. It wouldn't do to have one's spouse or children poring over these tomes, so for now, tuck them away in some clever hiding place. When you are older, and presumably wiser, you can dig the letters out again. Grandchildren will be delighted to read them, and in the name of family history you (devil, you) will, of course, pass them along. By then, the letter will be considered thrilling and will serve as testament to your long and terribly exciting life.

Magazines. (See also Catalogues, Mail.) Accumulating magazines (as in piles and piles of) is the ultimate guilt trip. People keep magazines because they "have to read something in there." Having made this declaration, the magazine gets tossed into the To Read pile, which grows unabated until there are magazines and/or trade journals all over the place. All this time, there is a little wad of guilt working on you . . . "gotta find the time to read that . . . gotta find the time to read that . . . gotta. . . ." It never stops, and of course you don't have the time to read all of that stuff, but instead of admitting that, you hang on to the fantasy by keeping more magazines than you ever needed to know about, much less, read. Everywhere you look are reminders of your *reading*, which you feel compelled to do, *one day soon.* One day soon almost never rolls around, and since subscriptions continue to flow into your home or office unchecked, it's akin to trying to plug Hoover Dam with your pinkie. *Face it, you're never going to catch up with all of that reading!* Only when you come to accept that undeniable fact will you be able to effectively deal with those piles of magazines. If you've already got a serious backlog, start by tossing out *all* of the magazines that are more than six months old. Don't even look at the captions on the cover or at the table of contents. If you do, you'll weaken, and convinced that you have to read just that one article, you'll move that magazine from one to another sacred pile, accomplishing absolutely nothing. So, just look at the dates and start tossing. Next, look at the remaining magazines and check for those articles that you *must* read. Cut the article out, staple it, and toss it in a To Read bin or basket. Now throw the rest of the magazine (mostly

Your magazine "collection" should be kept to a minimum; those you do keep on hand can be neatly stored on a shelf in these upright magazine organizers.

JBL Graphics, Montrose, California

advertisements anyway) away. Tomorrow, over coffee, pull out an article and read it. Now you've got at least a prayer of catching up. As new magazines come in, continue to scan them and clip only the articles that you want to read. Keep the articles in a large basket near your favorite reading spot, be it your desk, bed, the kitchen table, or your easy chair. When the basket gets full, throw something in the basket away (you can read it first) before you put anything else into the basket. This procedure should be employed consistently and is otherwise known as the In and Out Inventory Rule. It goes like this: Something new comes in, something old goes out. Keep this rule in mind as you reassess your current subscription list. Are you getting some magazines that you've really outgrown? If so, drop the subscription. And whatever you do, never, never, pick up a new subscription unless you let an old one go. Finally, carry some articles with you in your handbag, briefcase, or car. You never know when you're going to be stuck waiting, and twenty minutes of reading here and there puts that waiting time to good use, chipping away at that guilt-grabbing monster — your To Read pile.

Mail. Mail is an inescapable fact of life. Think about it. When you're young, you don't get any mail, and your life hums along quite happily without it. Sometime in your twenties, mail starts to become a constant in your life, bringing letters, bills, catalogues, magazines, and assorted charitable solicitations. As you hit your thirties, suddenly mail becomes very important, with the daily deluge of paper obligations increasing ominously with the years. Finally, old age finds mail dwindling again, just when everybody would like to find a letter or two in the box. At the peak of this life mail curve, you can feel totally overwhelmed. Once this mindset kicks in, you may find yourself (gasp!) not opening the mail at all! Mail, multiplying relentlessly and viciously—like the creepy pods in *The Invasion of the Bodysnatchers*—now begins to take over.

At the office, mail is delivered from a cart that is pushed by an abnormally cheerful person who is smiling because any minute now, the mail will be out of that cart and on *your* desk! Sometimes this horrific ritual takes place two or three times each day. Taking a day off from work to stay home doesn't help. You find yourself padding out to the mailbox in your slippers, and jeez, there's *more* of the stuff!

Mail can sneak up on almost anybody, and once you haven't had the time to take care of yesterday's or last week's mail, you *know* in your heart of hearts that there is *no way* you are going to be able to take care of the paper (mail) that gets dumped on you today. Before you know it, the stuff is piling up everywhere—on the desk, your dining room table, on the top of the refrigerator, in the entry, and next to the bed. A quick look at it reveals papers of every description, from bills to magazines. In fact the Table of Contents of this book might just be a list of the type of stuff that's sitting in your piles of unopened mail. Before you use this book to help you decide what to do with and how to file those papers, you have to first open the mail and find out what's in the envelope. Here's how to get past those piles of mail today and to deal with the mail from this point on:

First, accept the fact that if you don't do anything else with the mail, at least you should *sort* the incoming proliferation. Then, if and when you actually decide to *do* something about all of that postmarked paperwork, at least it will be waiting for you in an organized manner.

Begin with the obvious:

Open the Mail: This sounds simple enough, but as with all things simple, there is always somebody who either ignores it or does it wrong. Open the mail with a letter opener and pull the letter or bill or whatever out of the envelope. *Do not put it back into the envelope!* I see people folding and unfolding things dozens of times over just so they can keep the paper inside the envelope it arrived in. They do this repeatedly until they finally decide to *do* something with it. This is a waste of time, and that extra outer envelope is good for absolutely nothing except wasting space. So remove the letter or bill, throw away the envelope it came in, along with any other junk inserts, and if there is a return envelope (such as those enclosed for bills), attach it to the paper (letter or bill) with a paper clip and lay it flat on your desk. Now would be a good time to throw away junk mail, but if you can't bring yourself to part with it yet, go on to the next step:

Sort the Mail: Sorting the mail relies heavily on the Four-Step Paper Processing System explained in Part One. You'll want to sort your mail every day into those four categories:

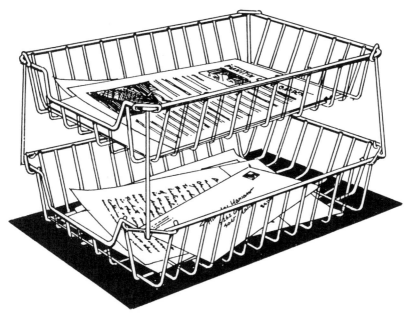

Wire baskets make it easy for you to see at a glance what you have to do and to pay.

Shu Yamamoto

To Do

To Pay

To File

To Read

Then, of course, there's the trash basket. Put it to good use. (Refer back to pages 12-18 for a blow-by-blow description of exactly how to sort the mail.)

If no one helps you with the mail, and if you are operating from home and don't have a desk or lots of filing cabinets, you can set up your sorting station in a portable rolling cart. Simply set up a basket in the cart for each category (these baskets are quite large, and slide out easily so you can take them over to your work area as needed). The cart can always be stored in a closet when not in use and pulled next to the bed, dining table, or your chair when you need to sort the mail or do some household paperwork. Permanent files can be stored in the closet in transfile boxes that can be purchased inexpensively from an office supply store.

Whether you are working at a desk or the dining room table, remember that sorting your mail into these four categories doesn't mean that you have "to do" it or "to pay" it or even "to file" it immediately; you merely need to sort it in order to do whatever it is you are supposed to do with it later.

This sort-the-mail concept will come in especially handy when you need to find something in a hurry. You won't have to sift through every piece of paper in the house or office; you will only have to go through the stack in the appropriate bin. For example, if you have an impatient bill collector on the phone, and you need to lay your hands on that unpaid bill (of course, we know you *intend* to pay it; you just haven't done so *yet*), all you have to do is look through your To Pay basket and, presto zippo, you will find it in one fourth the time it would have taken for you to rummage through *all* of the papers that had come in the recent batches of mail.

Sorting and effectively dealing with the mail is a critical component of paper management. You can let your mail become a monument to clutter, or you can become its master if you'll just open it, sort it, and throw a goodly portion of it away the minute you get it. Deal with what's left regularly — whether it's good news or bad — and you'll be able to keep yourself out of the middle of the mail muddle once and for all.

You can also reduce the volume of mail substantially by eliminating the junk. Write to the Direct Mail Marketing Association and tell them you want the junk mail stopped, and they will arrange to stop your name from being sold to most large mailing-list companies, which should reduce your junk mail influx substantially. Just think of all the trees and personal time you will save by heading off all that junk mail at the pass. Write to: Mail Preference Service, Direct Mail Marketing Association, 6 East Forty-third St. New York NY 10017.

Manuscripts. If you're a writer and have manuscripts you need to keep, your best bet is to tie them with string or a rubber band (although rubber bands are not great since they disintegrate) and store them in box on a shelf. Once your book has been published, assuming it is published in a form that is close to the original manuscript, you may be able to get rid of the manuscript. You will need to check with your publisher and, possibly, your attorney before you destroy this document, particularly if you have information in your book that might possibly be challenged legally at some future date. If your manuscript is smaller — say, the original article that was submitted and published in a magazine or newspaper — it can be filed either under Manuscripts (with a possible subtitle, such as Magazines or Newspapers), or it can be filed under the name of the publication (such as *Los*

Angeles Times Manuscripts). These should be purged every year or so and either tossed or moved to storage, unless you plan to sell them again to other markets. If resale or self-syndication is your reason for hanging on to the original works, keep only a few working copies on hand to send out; don't give in to making dozens of copies of one piece unless you are prepared to sit down right then and send dozens out (for resale).

Maps. Some people keep maps from all of their trips. Then they try to stuff them into the filing cabinets, into boxes, bureau drawers, or under the bed. Other maps get used from time to time but once unfolded, never seem to get folded back up again, so they wind up a torn mess in place of what should be a map. Maintaining an inventory of maps — for sentimental reasons or otherwise — can pose a serious challenge to reason. You say you still have that London subway map to remind you of your trip to London ten years ago on your anniversary? Does it take a subway map to jog those memories? And you've got that map of Arizona from when you took the family in the RV to the Grand Canyon . . . gee, wasn't that a super trip! Yup, it sure was, but I don't see what that old battered map has to do with how great the trip was . . . is there a picture of the canyon on the map? I can't believe that you need a map to jog your memories of this trip either. And *if* you ever do get back to London or to the Grand Canyon, you can always pick up another map from the subway station attendant (in England) or (for other maps) you can visit your Auto Club or a local gas station prior to your trip. It's silly to keep maps as mementos; they take up a lot of space and are a pain in the you-know-what to keep folded. So unless you are a truck driver who constantly criss-crosses the country in an eighteen-wheeler for a living, you can probably get along just fine without a drawer full of maps.

And for those of you who really are on the road regularly, you might want to purchase a portable storage box with a handle to store your maps neatly either in the trunk or on the floor in the back. Check your local variety stores or a full-service office supply store for a box that will accommodate the maps you need. Then just keep that one pertinent map that you are using in the front of the car (in the glove box or console), use the box to hold the other maps, which you can pull out and store as needed.

Master File. (See pages 45-46.)

Medical Records. Medical records and invoices should be set up in files located in your Financial section if you have one — since, let's face it, if you are going to doctors and dentists, you are probably spending money. And if it isn't your own actual cash, it comes from your insurer; thus your insurance files should be in the Financial section because of the financial aspects as well as the complexity of it all. As always, if you have only a few household files, these records can be filed alphabetically within your general files. Typical Medical files include a separate medical category for dental work (if warranted). Here are some sample files for a family of three:

Medical—John

Medical—Myrna

Medical—Susie

Medical—Dental—Susie

Since the bills you get from doctors often indicate the diagnosis as well, you may want to keep these, particularly if you are under long-term treatment. Otherwise, once each year add the total financial outlay for tax purposes and transfer these records to storage. Check with your accountant, but chances are, if you paid by check (and you still have your statements) you can throw away the original bills at the end of each year.

Other information about your medical history can also be kept in this file, but articles and general information about health and health-related issues should probably be kept in another file such as Health Information. Otherwise your medical file will become too cluttered to deal with easily. When you move your paid bills out of this file to storage at the end of the year, leave the pertinent medical history records in the file for reference whenever it may be needed. One final tip: Make a note on the inside of your Medical file folder of your insurance account number. That way, if there is an emergency, and someone else has to act in your behalf at the hospital, they can pull your medical file and get the critical insurance information at a glance. (Keep this number in your wallet as well on a card that also lists who to notify in case of emergency.)

Meeting Records. Meeting records, including agendas, minutes, and committee reports from Board of Directors meetings or from fundraising event committee meetings and the like, usually need to be kept in chronological order. Along with the minutes and reports, these meetings often generate other back-up material and notes that are pertinent to that meeting and possibly to future meetings. All of these papers can be kept in order in a three-ring binder divided by either months or by the meeting dates. If you like, you can add further divisions for the different committee reports such as treasurer's reports, fund-raising or awards committee reports, and so forth.

The binder provides a portable paper storage system that allows you to conveniently carry last month's meeting records with you to this month's meeting. If you need to refer to something that happened at a previous meeting during a current meeting, the binder provides an immediate resource. (Keep the agenda for each meeting filed on top of the other backup material from the meeting. It serves as a sort of table of meeting contents for you.) If you leave the board or the committee dissolves after the charitable event has been successfully concluded, you can pass your complete set of records over to the next person or to the office of the charitable cause via this one large, but simple and organized binder.

Mementos. Paper memories invade almost everybody's life to some degree. It is important to look at the amount of paper you are keeping for memory's sake before you try to figure out what to do with it all. If you are keeping every greeting card, every piece of paper your child drags home from school, and all of your notes and term papers from your college days, you are overdoing it. There is no magic way to store cartons upon cartons of this stuff, so there's nothing I can tell you that will help you organize it all. On the other hand, if you are willing to do the sensible thing and get rid of some of the overload, there are then several things you can do with the remaining mementos that you have selected as bona fide pieces of reminiscence about your life. Putting mementos in your filing system is really not advisable, since these papers and cards are often either bulky or odd sized. Besides, who wants to "pull a file" to go through mementos? A better solution for storage is to keep them in boxes or albums. You can purchase fabric-covered boxes, attractive hat boxes or, if you wish, fireproof strongboxes to hold some of these paper memories. You can also purchase boxes that are acid free, which adds to the life of your papers over the years and helps prevent deterioration. Albums are also a good forum for mementos, and you can either make your own with a three-ring binder, and sheet protectors, and photo sleeves purchased at the stationery store, or you can use the traditional photo or scrap album and mount your items with mounting corners. If you are one of those people who are going to put it all in an album "someday soon," you can even store the papers in plastic sweater boxes by category in the meantime. For instance, you can put a selection of your child's special pieces of art in one box, and your love letters in another box. You can find boxes and albums in variety stores, department stores, office supply stores, and photo stores. If you want to use acid-free materials and none of these sources have them, check with your local museum or historical society to see if they can provide you with the name of a supplier of these materials.

There really is a place in everyone's life for mementos. But take care to select only the most significant specimens for your memories, and make sure you put them in some semblance of order so that they can be effectively stored. Remember to make them accessible as well, since what's the point of carefully keeping mementos if you can't get to them to reminisce when the mood hits you?

Memos. Memos are written for a variety of reasons. There's the impulse reason. You think of something, and connected to the thought is an automatic knee-jerk response, "gotta write a memo to that effect." Everybody needs to know what you are thinking, so they get your memo. Then there's the traditional CYA (cover-your-ahem) memo that is written to prove that you did or said this or that. Everybody gets this one too, since one can't be too careful these days. Then there's the "commando" memo. As in, please do this or that, and have it on my desk yesterday. If you are writing these memos, you're a commander/boss of some sort, and these memos prove it, yesirree. Whatever the reason, all in all, there are billions of memos generated every day, which is at least a few million more than is necessary. But you can't throw them away, because the person who wrote it might find out, and then you'd be in trouble for sure. So make up a binder for memos only and file them in chronological order, divided by months. If you regularly receive memos from some VIPs, you may want to break the binder down by person:

Mr. Bigwig—January
        February
        March

Mr. Bigwig, Jr.—January
        February
        March

and so on. If your superiors are really memo dependent, you may have to carry this binder to meetings so that you can refer to them. You can flip to the memo and say something like, "as you recommended in your excellent memo of January 14 regarding our strategic planning. . . ."

If you are a superior and would like to see fewer memos in your life, start by writing fewer yourself, and when you do write them, don't automatically have your secretary copy everybody in the world. When you do that, you have taken one piece of paper and multiplied it by, say, twenty (you're sending it to twenty people); out of those twenty knuckleheads, at least a few of them are going to sit down and knock out a memo to you in response to your memo—even if no response was required! Now *they're* going to send it out to twenty people, plus you, and out of those twenty people a few are going to respond to *this* memo. .... You get the picture. So if everybody would write just two fewer memos this week and every week thereafter, by the end of the year, the amount of paper that gets copied, shuffled around, reacted to and filed, will be reduced by at least a few thousand pieces, saving you and the company time and money.

Move your memo binders from previous years into storage. I'd like to say toss them, but that's too reactionary for most people, so I won't say it. Instead, you can pass the binders on to the next sap that moves into your job.

Minutes. (See Meeting Records.)

Miscellaneous. Miscellaneous is a title that goes onto cabinets, drawers, piles, and files. "Oh, that's miscellaneous stuff in there," or "File it in miscellaneous." The fact is, these piles and files are generated when you can't figure out what to do with something. I know this, and you know this. Things are sucked into miscellaneous chambers, to be lost and forgotten forever. Or people spend inordinate amounts of time sifting through the huge miscellaneous piles and files, looking for something, because "maybe it's in miscellaneous." Do what you can to get rid of most of the miscellaneous departments in your paper life—from files to entire cabinets—and put things where they really belong. If you can't entirely lick the problem by finding a secure categorical place for everything, allow yourself one general miscellaneous file. Check it once a quarter, and if it has more than fifteen pieces of paper in it, move the excess to someplace sensible, or throw it away.

Along with this allowance of one miscellaneous file (in the general files), you may find yourself with a sprinkling of additional miscellaneous files in your system. Here are some ways to handle those must-have miscellaneous matters.

You can keep miscellaneous client name files in alphabetically marked files within each letter just for that purpose. For instance, suppose your client files have five files organized by client name under the *A*, plus some miscellaneous files. Here is how you might organize the section:

A—(These hold miscellaneous *A* names of clients who are only temporary or who generate minimal paperwork and don't warrant their own file.)

Adams, James

Anderson, Mary

Andrews, Bill

Astin, Thelma

Axon, Thomas & Co.

These are examples of possible substantial files.

If your alphabetical files contain more than just client name files, your miscellaneous needs would very likely be quite different. Instead you might have a general miscellaneous client file under *C* marked Clients — Miscellaneous. In this general system, you will only have scattered miscellaneous files rather than miscellaneous files behind each alphabetical letter. Common miscellaneous files are:

Correspondence — Miscellaneous

Expenses — Miscellaneous

Travel Information — Miscellaneous

Remember, whatever you have as "miscellaneous," try to limit the amount of paper you assign to this category — otherwise it becomes a dumping ground for papers you don't know how to file. And if you assign specific categories to miscellaneous (such as "Correspondence"), be sure to label the file with the category first and miscellaneous second: *Correspondence — Miscellaneous*, not *Miscellaneous — Correspondence*.

Finally, weed these out regularly. It's amazing how easily miscellaneous can become trash six months after it gets dumped into the I-don't-know-what-to-do-with-this-paper file, otherwise known as *Miscellaneous*.

Mortgage. File these payment stubs in your Financial section under *M* for mortgage or with the house records under House — Mortgage. You have the same choice if you only have a general file, *H* or *M*.

Mutual Funds. (See Investments.)

Newspapers. Here's a pop quiz for you: What are the first four letters in the word, newspapers?

Gosh, you're smart. That's right: N, E, W, S.

Without exception, newspapers should be read immediately and tossed or recycled. Stacks of newspapers draw bugs and are a fire hazard. Two days after the newspapers arrive, the information is not news anymore. About all the paper is good for is lining the bottom of the bird cage or wrapping up garbage. If you're worried that you're missing something in that stack of newspapers you've got piled up, try this oldie but goodie: *No news is good news*. Amen.

Notes. Note nuts go around writing notes to themselves and everybody else unlucky enough to be within note range. Notes are jotted down on scrap paper, on the backs of business cards, on notepads, and on yellow legal pads. Eventually these notes are scattered all over the place, with new notepads and legal pads started by the dozens. Then, of course, you need to allocate time to organize, reevaluate, and rewrite your notes to yourself. Lordy. Give it a rest, why don'tcha? Nothing much is going to get done while you are searching for your notes. You'll spend twenty minutes trying to find the right notes, another twenty trying to decipher your hand-writing, and even more time rewriting those notes. All this before any action whatsoever has been taken.

The best way to deal with uncontrollable note clutter is to gather the notes up, throw them away, and start clean. Then keep *one* To Do list in one book or on one notepad and make sure it is easy to find by giving it a special spot (such as a basket by the phone or a drawer near your desk). Personal reflections should be kept in a journal for your eyes only and should not be mixed in with other daily notes and lists. You can set up a notebook that serves the sole function of holding notes. You can even divide your notebook by allocating one section for To Do lists, one section for To Buy lists, one section for Grocery lists, one section for Reminder lists, one section for Great Ideas, and one section for Affirmations. Whatever suits your note needs. Used as an addition to your daily planner or calendar, this notebook can help you keep your thoughts together so that you can act on them whenever you wish. Just remember that you have a notebook for your notes, so that the next time you find yourself reaching for a scrap of paper or a new notepad to make a note, give your hand a little smack and use your notebook instead.

Office Supplies. Office supplies, from paper clips to forms and stationery, call for a central holding station. This applies to the corporate office as well as to the home office. Having supplies scattered hither and yon only makes for inaccurate inventory judgments resulting in an under- or overabun-dance of the supplies that you need. Establish a cabinet or bookshelf area that will hold your office supplies. If there are several people using the supplies, the storage should be as centrally located as possible.

Stationery, and filing folders, and other filing supplies can be stored in their boxes on a shelf. Small items such as pens, pencils, paper clips, and the like can be stored in clearly labeled bins. With bins, you eliminate collapsing stacks, since the bin holds everything, stacked or not. Whatever you do, don't assign filing cabinet drawer space to hold office supplies. If you have other cabinet space and have just a few items, you might be able to store them in your desk, or you can invest in a rolling basket system.

At home, this basket system can be stored in the closet and pulled out when you need to use the supplies for paying bills or answering correspondence. A dining room buffet or a section of the linen closet can also provide excellent home storage for office supplies.

If you have a desk, keep a supply of stationery, pens, pencils, paper clips, rubber bands, and so on in the desk. The stationery can be kept in the file drawer in hanging file folders or on top of your desk in metal stationery trays. The smaller items can be contained neatly in your desk drawer with cutlery trays or other drawer dividers. Keep only a reasonable supply in your desk, since keeping too much in your desk can lead to clutter that will actually impede efficiency.

It is important to check all of your office supplies before you store them or order more. Outdated rubber stamps, stationery, business cards, and other items that you never use should be tossed out (the stationery might be cut into scratch paper). You'll save money by keeping your office supply inventory lean and mean, since cabinets full of office-supply clutter often result in misplaced supplies and, as a result, needlessly reordered items.

Organizational Chart. The organizational chart can be a valuable working tool or a piece of trash, depending on how you look at it and what your position is in the company. The chart, via a series of connecting boxes with names in them, lets you know, on paper, who the top dogs are. As if you didn't already know. Still, there might be times when the corporate bases seem loaded but nobody really knows who's on first. Whip out your trusty organizational chart for this information. The chart also lets you know with distressing clarity what your chances are of advancing to any meaningful position. Simply look at the chart and 1) see if you are even on the bloody thing; then 2) count how many people are ahead of you. Theoretically, this will give you a game plan for mowing down those people who are before you on your way to the top. Of course you may not care one whit about the chart because you're not on it, don't have a prayer of ever getting on it, and couldn't care less, because this place is just a stopover on your way to a much better life. Whatever your thoughts on the organizational chart, maybe you should slide it under your desk blotter for easy reference or file it in your desk drawer (with your action files, for quick and easy access). If someone asks you who is in charge of whom or what, this chart may provide your only clue to an answer. If you throw the chart away, when somebody asks you a chart-related question and you answer it by saying, "I dunno," they're going to know you don't give a bunny's behind about it all. Attitude news (as in "she's got a bad attitude") travels viciously fast along the office grapevine. So listen to me. Hang on to the chart. Replace it with new ones when new ones are issued. Make changes on the chart as people are added or subtracted from the firm. And every now and then, when it's called for, refer to your organizational chart and act like it is a meaningful thing to do by flashing a great big smile that says you care.

Passport. Put this in your safety deposit box, in a strongbox at home, or in your Important Documents file.

Pet Papers. Even pets generate paperwork. If they are pedigreed, there's the paperwork that attests to the fact that your little precious is born of some grand couple and is considered superior to a goodly portion of the rest of the run-of-the-mill animals in the neighborhood. You may have paperwork showing registration or city licensing, and you'll probably, at one time or another, collect vet bills that you've been obliged to pay. Unless you have a menagerie, one file is generally all that's necessary to hold your pets' papers. You can title the file however you like (in the general files). You can preface it with Pet, Animals, or you can just use your pet's name:

Animals — Fido and Fritz

Fido and Fritz

Pets — Fido and Fritz

If you have lots and lots of animals, add files as required. You needn't keep vet bills unless you're in the breeding business or have an animal for moneymaking purposes. And once an expired license has been replaced by a new one, you can eliminate the outdated papers as well. When a pet dies, you may find it easier to bite the bullet and throw the paperwork away. Unless you need it for tax purposes, keeping the memory of a beloved pet in your current files can be unnecessarily distressing. Instead, keep any mementos of your pet with your other mementos.

Phone Messages. Phone messages get written down on all manner of paper — scraps of paper, pink phone message slips, and other assorted forms and notepads. If someone is handling this chore (taking your phone messages) for you, you may have mixed feelings about how it's being done. Maybe they don't do a good job of getting the information down correctly.

Or maybe they're rude to the caller. These are all issues that can be resolved by getting an answering machine rather than a human being. This lets *you* take the information down as it comes off the machine and allows the machine to be cold and impersonal. How phone messages are handled is probably a book in itself, but what happens to those pieces of paper that the information is recorded on can probably be handled briefly here.

First, try to eliminate messages hastily written on odd scraps of paper and go instead for uniformity. Get the pink phone message pads or better yet, get the phone message pads that automatically give you a carbon of the message when you write one out. This is a real lifesaver for those times when you have lost the original and need to know the caller's number or need to know when the caller originally called you. You can simply refer back through the carbons that stay in chronological order on the pad. (Your office supply store has these.)

Next, establish a "message center." In the office, have everyone drop the messages into a specific box on your desk or credenza. Demand that they stop taping the messages on you chair (they do this because your desk is so full of papers that they know the phone message will become buried and therefore ignored).

At home, you can make a message center with a box or (be careful here), a bulletin board. Although I am, in general, vehemently opposed to bulletin boards (for a reminder of why I hate the things, turn to Bulletin Boards, pages 51-52), in this case they can work, but only so long as you and everyone else can resist the almost overwhelming urge to start sticking all kinds of other nonsense on the board (snapshots of Fido, postcards, etc.).

Once you've trained everybody (including yourself), to put the messages in one spot, you need to look at the reality of how you return your phone calls. I've worked with more people than I can count who, for some perverse reason, keep *hundreds* of these call slips, knowing full well that they can't possibly return all of those calls. The pile grows unmercifully for months at a time. The proud pile owner steadfastly refuses to let go of these piles of paper, which are usually invading every nook and cranny of the desk and office. "I need these," and "I have to go over these," are two common refrains heard as the perpetrator rushes to protect those call slips. Meanwhile, a new blizzard of call slips land on the desk adding to the proliferation every day.

If you've got these stacks all over the place, it's probably time to get off this silly paper habit. You may have to do it cold turkey. Have someone else go through the messages and tell them to *throw away everything that is more than two weeks old.* Don't try to do this yourself. You won't last five minutes before you'll start telling yourself why you have to keep these

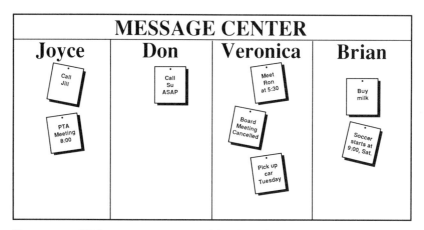

MESSAGE CENTER

Joyce	Don	Veronica	Brian

Call Jill

Call Su ASAP

Meet Ron at 5:30

Buy milk

PTA Meeting 8:00

Board Meeting Cancelled

Soccer starts at 9:00, Sat.

Pick up car Tuesday

You can establish a message center with a bulletin board and some colored tape. Set it up in a central area, near the main phone system if possible. At home keep it near the phone in the central living area — in the kitchen or the family room, for instance.

JBL Graphics, Montrose, California

things. As it is, it will take a heroic effort on your part to allow someone else to do it for you. But let's fact it, if you haven't returned a call in over two weeks, by now that person probably doesn't want to hear from you.

Next, call the people on the remaining call slips (the last two weeks' worth). Spend two full days doing it if that's what it takes. Once you've caught up, set aside time every day to *return your calls!* As you return each call, mark the slip if you want the caller's phone number added to your Rolodex (let someone else actually do the transferring); if not, throw the slip away! If you can't stand to throw the slip away and are falling back on the old "it's a potential customer" excuse, store the slips in a large covered box on the floor or in your credenza in the office. This will keep these pieces of paper contained and off your desk. Once every eight weeks or so, close your eyes and throw out everything in the box without looking at the slips you are tossing. With a little luck, you'll eventually wean yourself from this useless paper collecting habit, and you'll be able to throw these unreturned call slips directly into the trash rather than using the storage box as an intermediate step to curing yourself.

Phone Numbers. Phone numbers and addresses enter our lives via any number of avenues. Scraps of paper, business cards, and personal mail — all carry important phone numbers and addresses needed for future reference. Almost everyone has lost an important phone number or misplaced a vital address at one time or another. To eliminate the frantic scramble for a misplaced phone number or address, keep your phone numbers on a Rolodex that's large enough to accommodate your needs.

Some people keep all of their phone numbers in an address book. This only works if changes and additions are rarely made. Otherwise, the address book turns into an unreadable mess, with names and numbers scratched out and new entries squeezed in along the side of the page. A Rolodex system eliminates this confusion since it is easy to add names and make changes by inserting a new card in the proper alphabetical order. There are all types of Rolodex systems available, small and large (some are even fairly attractive), but I think the large wheel system is best. Smaller systems may look prettier, but they fill up in no time; before you know it, you've run out of room and the cards start popping up and off of the tracks. The large wheel holds at least a zillion phone numbers, you can staple business cards right on to the Rolodex card, it's easy to use and to find information at a glance, and it lasts forever.

As you collect phone numbers (whether it's via business cards or tiny scraps of papers that you hastily scribble information on), throw them into a small basket or container. Periodically, you (or someone else) can sit down and type up the cards for the Rolodex. You can also staple business cards directly to the Rolodex card. If the business card is a bit too big, trim a piece off the top or bottom of the card and save yourself the work of manually transferring the information onto the Rolodex card. If you need to scrounge up a number before it gets put on the Rolodex, you'll know it isn't lost. It will be in the basket waiting to be transferred. Weed out your Rolodex at least once a year, eliminating names and numbers that you don't need. Weeding out your Rolodex is something that can also easily be done in five-minute chunks; simply mark where you stopped by putting a paper clip on that card. Then when you have another five minutes, go through a few more cards, starting at the paper-clipped card. If you're required to listen to long-winded bores on the phone, you can make that time more productive by doing your five minute Rolodex weeding while your caller is running off at the mouth.

A functioning Rolodex with only pertinent phone numbers and addresses can work wonders for your daily professional life, putting vital information at your fingertips in an organized manner. For that matter, if you keep your personal phone numbers and addresses in good order on a Rolodex, it might just perk up your social life as well!

Photocopies. Photocopies of papers should be handled according to the type of paper at hand—is it financial, does it go into the general file, and so on. But before you hit that button on the photocopy machine, ask yourself if you really need to have and/or disburse ten copies of that memo about the office Christmas party. Maybe, gee, since it's a party, you could mention it to your secretary and two other guys and ask them to spread the word, and maybe, just maybe, the word will get out without adding ten more pieces of paper to the mountains of paper already shifting around the office. Any maybe you don't need another copy of that cover letter saying that something you've been expecting is herewith enclosed. And just because you thought that cartoon was such a gas does not mean that four of your relatives and two of your friends will agree when they get your photocopy. And just because you don't have anything better to do than read articles, copy them, and send them out to friends (and maybe enemies) doesn't mean that the recipients will be appreciative of your efforts—all enhanced and made possible in the first place by that danged photocopying machine. Think about it. What did we do before those machines? Answer: We used carbon copies only when necessary because correcting the copies was a real pain in the you-know-what. Today you should operate with more or less the same attitude. Photocopy only when necessary, because all that extra paper—I don't care who gets it—is a pain in the you-know-what.

Photographs. Some people take to photographs like bees to honey. They run around snapping pictures of everything from Grandpa's seventieth birthday party to the new bushes in the backyard. They're addicted to cameras. The finger that pushes the button starts to twitch if it doesn't get to click-click a camera every time the shutterbug turns around. These people have pictures up the proverbial wazoo. If this sounds like you, consider this: *Photographs don't do anybody any good if they can't be seen.*

Of course everybody *plans* to put their zillions of photographs in an album (or two or three or twenty albums), but they never do. I once met a woman who put her photos into albums the minute she brought them home from the developers (she had sixty albums). I was so thunderstruck at the thought that someone could actually be *that* efficient that all I could say to the woman was, "Aren't you wonderful?" Most people don't do that, and so, naturally, the photos don't get seen, much less enjoyed. If you've got photos that need to be organized, use these guidelines to clear up any backlog you might have and to keep your photographs in good order from now on:

Declare a Moratorium: If you've got several years of unsorted photos, spend ninety minutes each week working on the project. Don't take any more pictures until you have organized the backlog you already have!

Preserve the Past: Old family heirloom photos deserve priority since, left untended, they can deteriorate badly. You'll also want to check with family members for missing information about the people in the photos so that you can record that information on or with the photo.

Critic's Corner: Look at your photos critically, with an eye to eliminate all but the best. Get rid of shots that are blurred or fuzzy. Toss those unflattering shots that make you cringe every time you look at them. Also consider getting rid of those photos that are dumb, boring, or mediocre (you don't need a shot of Dad talking to Mom). Definitely get rid of pictures of people that you no longer recognize. Throw or give away duplicates.

Label Everything: Mark photos with a date and a number. Put the same date and number on the corresponding negative. Store the negatives in an envelope and mark the dates and numbers on the front of the envelopes. This is a lot of work, and there's no point in doing it if you are fairly certain that you'll never make reprints. If you think reprints are unnecessary, it's not a sin to toss the negatives.

Categorize: As you're editing your photos, you may want to organize them by category. For example, Vacations, Special Events, Pets, Sports, Family. You can also make chronological categories according to periods in your life, such as Childhood, College, or New York, California (for the time you lived in each of those places).

Storage: Once the photos are organized, you can store them in large manila envelopes, fabric-covered or acid-free boxes, hat boxes, or plastic shoe or sweater boxes with labels. You can also put them in traditional albums or in albums that you can make yourself with sheet protectors and photo sleeves that you can buy at the stationery store and then put into a three-ring binder. If you put the photos in albums, be sure to put them where everyone can go through them whenever they want.

Business Shots: Photographs such as product shots, photos for advertisements and brochures, head shots, and the like can be stored in manila envelopes in file folders titled Photographs followed by the photo's application. For example, you may have the following Photograph files:

Photographs — Ads, Christmas Catalogue

Photographs — Brochure, 1990

Photographs — Head Shots — Mr. Jackson

Photographs — Product Shots — Wacky Widget

If your business is photo intensive, you can also organize the photos into manila envelopes that are then placed in transfile boxes (thus saving space in the filing cabinet for other paperwork and files that may be needed on a daily or weekly basis. Take care of these photos as you would personal photos by at least noting the date and other pertinent facts on the manila envelope that holds the photos. And, once each year, go through the files and eliminate out-of-date photographs by saving only a selection of them for historical purposes (these can be stored in a box with other historical records).

Slide Shows: Sort out your slides just as ruthlessly as you would photos, using the same sorting principles. You can also sort them into slide "shows" and store each show in a carousel tray with a label (e.g., Amy's Eighth Birthday). These trays can be stored on shelves or on a closet floor or in a cabinet.

Documentation: From now on, when you bring the photos home, make sure you immediately identify the photo by noting who is in the photo, the location, and the year, as well as the ages of the people in the photo. You may think you will always remember all of the details of those photos, but you won't. The day will undoubtedly come when you find yourself holding up a photo in total bewilderment, wondering who on earth that person with the red hair is. Durned if I know. You won't know either fifteen years from now, so if you don't do anything else to organize your photos, at least start identifying them now so you won't be so befuddled later on.

Plans. Architectural blueprints are so oversized and bulky that they can be almost impossible to deal with. Unless you are in the building business, you probably don't have many sets of these, but what you do have is driving you crazy. The easiest thing to do with them is to roll them and store them either in an architect's bin (made expressly for this purpose) or, for an alternative that is dirt cheap, simply buy a smaller round lucite or plastic trash can and store the rolled plans in the can. You can put it in a corner or in a closet. Often plans don't need to be kept forever—plans for renovating the kitchen, for example, probably don't have to be kept for more than a year after the job is done. So you can consider throwing them away unless you feel you will be doing more work in the future and using those plans once again.

Political Information. If you are politically active, you may want to keep some resource information on the topic. The easy thing to do is to keep a file marked Politics and keep your material in that file. Remember, though, that much of what you receive in the mail on the subject you already know, and half of the rest of it does not represent the real world as you may know it. Political papers—whether they are pleas for money for a campaign or the latest information on why Candidate X should be elected—quickly become

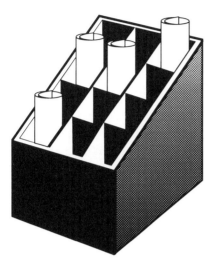

This heavy-duty corrugated organizer holds posters, plans, and other odd-sized papers that can be rolled and stored.

JBL Graphics, Montrose, California

dated, so you can dispense with a lot of them due to simple irrelevancy. My final word on the subject is that, unless you're planning to run for office yourself, you don't need most of those papers anyway.

Postcards. A supply of blank postcards is always useful to have on hand. Keep them nearby in your desk drawer or carry a few with you to jot quick notes to people during otherwise wasted waiting time. Unfortunately, for some mysterious reason many people also feel compelled to keep postcards that are sent them from friends and relatives. If they went to the trouble of sending this card from Europe, we should keep it, and besides that, there's a picture of the Eiffel Tower on the card. Gotta save it, right? Wrong. Read it and toss it. If you want to see the Eiffel Tower again, save your money and take your own trip.

If you still insist on saving all those postcards, about all you can do is put them in a box and store them on a shelf somewhere. You're hopeless.

Procedure Manuals. Procedure manuals serve a good purpose, particularly in companies where there is constant change or turnover in personnel. If your company or department is operating without the benefit of a procedure manual, and particularly if paperwork is getting lost or bogged down in the system, a procedure manual can be a worthwhile project to undertake. In order to put one together, someone needs to analyze every function individually and then analyze how those functions fit into your overall operational scheme. During this analysis, terrible glitches and stupid procedures are usually unearthed and brought to the attention of management who, with a great wailing and moaning, thump their chests and pound their desks, demanding that everybody shape up or ship out. Streamlined, efficient procedures for pushing paper are put into effect, the manual is written so nobody forgets how to do what it is they're supposed to be doing, and everything is beautiful for a while. When a new employee arrives on the scene, training that employee is made easier with the written help of the procedure manual. Eventually, however, procedures change for one reason or another (the business outgrows the procedure, new forms are introduced, some functions are subcontracted out, or an employee sets about sabotaging a procedure). When this happens, suddenly some part of the procedure manual becomes inaccurate and, therefore, outdated, which gives the people who were against the manual in the first place a great deal of satisfaction. Eventually, the manual is relegated to some lonely corner where it is ignored altogether, and procedures slowly fall apart or become as convoluted as they were before the manual's introduction.

To avoid this, it is imperative to understand that a procedure manual is never really finished. The original manual is the backbone where your company procedures are concerned, but it is only the backbone. Periodically, as the company grows and/or things change for that or other reasons, the procedure manual must be made to reflect those changes. Sometimes this means modifying only a paragraph or a sentence; sometimes it means revising several pages. Designate your most organized and efficient employee as the person who keeps the manual up to date. When there are changes in procedures, the old, out-of-date information is pulled and is replaced by new information. These updates are sent to anyone in the company who has a manual, and they are expected to at least follow minimal instructions, which in this case are to remove the old pages (tell them exactly which ones, so they can't screw it up) and replace them with the new pages that you are supplying. This all seems like needless paper pushing, and if your company or department is humming along like a well-tuned instrument, maybe it is. But if you don't know who is doing what and haven't a clue as to how they do it, and if things are getting delayed or mishandled on a regular basis, you need to take a good hard look at what a procedure manual can do for you. This is definitely one case where some extra paper can help you more than it can hurt you.

Real Estate. If you are the proud owner of properties other than your home, you will need to establish some Real Estate files. Most likely this will go into your Financial section if you have one, and if you have subdivided that section with another category of Investments, you may want to put real estate there. For example:

Financial — Investments

Real Estate — 321 Main

Or you may just want to file these files under Real Estate. Where several properties are involved, it is important to further clarify the file by listing the address of the property:

Real Estate — 321 Main

Once you have set up a file for each property, break that property's paperwork down into additional files only if the file becomes too bulky to work with. For example, you may want to put all of the escrow papers in one file:

Real Estate — 321 Main
           Escrow

You would then set up another file for any additional paperwork, such as tax paperwork and, if you rent the property out, rental information. Again, if that file becomes unwieldy (as is often the case in commercial properties), simply set up extra files by category. You can keep the property tax information in its own file if you want, for example. (This can often be a good idea anyway, particularly if you're inclined to misplace or forget about these all-important payments.)

You can weed these files out once each year, moving last year's tenant information, for example, into storage. Give your accountant and/or lawyer any necessary facts and figures for accounting and legal purposes and hang on to all of the real estate records (unless your accountant and/or attorney advises otherwise) until the property is sold.

Once the property is sold, retain your paperwork through the end of the tax year, then check with your accountant to see what records need to be retained and what can be tossed.

If you sell real estate or your holdings are exceptionally complex or diverse, you may want to also read the sections in this book on Contracts, Forms, Legal Documents, and Sales Prospects.

Reading Material. (See Magazines, Newspapers.)

Receipts. You can set up as many receipt files as you need, depending on how you view these pieces of paper. Again, this would go in your Financial section, if you have one, or you can just drop it into your General files if you have one simple system for all of your papers. These are some of the receipts that people traditionally drag home or back to the office:

Receipts — Auto Gasoline purchases

Receipts — Charge Account purchases (the charge slip)

Receipts — Department Store purchases

Receipts — Office Supply purchases

Receipts — Petty Cash purchases

Receipts — Postage

The best thing to do with these scraps of paper is to establish a drop site for them so that when you pull them out of your pocket or bag, you immediately put them in this area, eliminating the chances of losing or misplacing them. Set up a box of some kind (a cigar box is good) and just drop the receipts in the box (make sure you place the box in a convenient location).

Generally, most receipts are kept from cash purchases in the above areas. The reasons vary, and the method of handling all this paper can be a year-end mess requiring hours and hours of sorting, or it can be a task that takes only a few minutes each week, leaving you with all of your receipts automatically organized *before* tax time even gets here. Try these ideas on for size:

Charge Account Receipts: These are those obnoxious tissue slips that serve as our copy of the charge invoice on purchases made with credit cards. Put these in your receipt box, and once each month, pull them out and sort them by company, putting MasterCard in one stack, Visa in another, American Express in another. Do the same with any other credit card account receipts you have (such as your department store charge receipts). Next, compare them against your statement from the company. If it is listed correctly on the statement, you can *throw that tissue away.* There is no reason to keep it, because the information has been transferred to your statement. If you can't stand the thought of throwing these away, or if you want to keep it because you made an important notation on it (such as who you took to lunch) you can staple them to the back of the statement. But do not throw them into the file loose; it just adds confusion and invites more work at tax time. (For more on this, see Charge Accounts.)

Department Store Receipts: If you paid cash for clothing or household goods at a department store, there is no reason to keep this receipt unless you think you might return the item or unless it is somehow tax deductible. If it is tax deductible (unlikely), put it with your petty cash accounting (see next section for more on this). If it is not tax deductible, but you want to keep it to make sure you won't need to return the item, put it in a file marked Receipts—Department Stores. Make sure you write what the item is, if it isn't already noted on the receipt. Clean this file out periodically, tossing any receipts that you now know are for goods that you will not be returning.

Petty Cash: Much of the rest of your cash receipts can be handled by grouping them into petty cash. Use this petty cash system for tax-deductible cash purchases only. Here's how it works:

Put your receipts into a box designated for these tax deductible cash purchases. Periodically go through the box and separate the receipts by category. For example, the following categories might very well be in your petty cash box:

Auto Gas

Office Supplies $\Big\}$ Petty Cash

Postage

Once the receipts have been divided by category, add up each category to get a total amount of cash paid for that category. Enter this information on the front of a business-sized envelope and total the figures:

Auto Gas	21.50
Office Supplies	15.09
Postage	25.00
Total	61.59

Put the receipts inside the envelope and file the envelope in a Receipts—Petty Cash file. At tax time, simply add up the figures by category on the front of the envelope. These are now your tax-deductible cash expenses for the year. Not only does this simplify and streamline your cash accounting, it takes what could otherwise be an enormous chore at tax time (breaking out all of the cash receipts by category) and reduces it to a simple procedure that will take less than an hour to calculate.

Taking petty cash a step further, you can "reimburse" yourself every time you calculate your petty cash outlay. Simply have a check issued to you—even if it means writing it yourself—for the total cash outlay in this case, $61.59). On the check stub, enter the category breakdown that appears on the front of the envelope, and on the front of the envelope add a notation indicating the check number and date paid. The cash disbursement is then added to your monthly bookkeeping records, and the petty cash envelope is filed in the event that it need to be pulled as proof of purchase (for the IRS). Your cash disbursement monthly records would simply list how you spent your money for legitimate tax-deductible expenses, and it would break it down by category. Included in this breakdown would be your petty cash expenses (in this case for auto gas, office supplies, and postage). These figures would be tallied and transferred at tax time (rather than going to the envelopes), and the petty cash envelopes would be kept as back-up proof of your expenses only.

Recipes. Recipes come to us from cookbooks, magazines, and newspapers. Cookbooks are easy to deal with if you only buy books that you intend to use, and then you actually *use* them. Recipes that you clip from magazines and newspapers are another matter. And the time-honored, much-loved recipes from Grandma and your mother-in-law only add to the recipe clutter. The first commandment of recipes is that, unless you are going to put your clipped recipes *in order* and follow that up by actually *using* those recipes on a fairly regular basis, *don't clip them in the first place!* Because if you do, that one bulging drawer of yellowing, never used recipes will multiply to fill two or three drawers that you could be using to store something else that you really *use.*

For all those recipes that you *do* want to use, you can make your own personal cookbook. Buy a large three-ring binder (get the type that salespeople use for display and presentation purposes). This binder is encased in plastic so that salespeople can slip a piece of paper with information onto the front of the binder. It's going to allow *you* to keep the thing clean. Next, buy a box of clear plastic sheet protectors. Both the binders and sheet protectors are available at your office supply store. Organize your recipes by category, such as Breads, Entrees, Appetizers, Desserts, and so forth. Then slip each recipe into a sheet protector and staple or tape it to the black piece of paper inside the plastic. If your recipes are written on two sides of the paper or an index card, simply remove the black insert sheet from inside the sheet protector and staple the recipe directly onto the plastic. All you have to do is flip the sheet protector over to see the rest of the recipe. This binder also makes it easy for you to keep the photos of the recipe *with* the recipe—even if you have to use two pages. Just put the

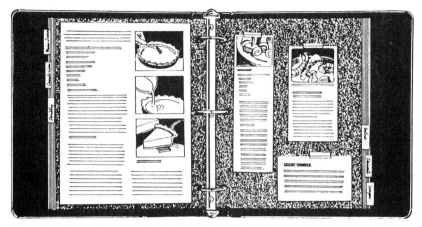

Your family recipes never looked better. This binder system is guaranteed to keep all of your recipes in order and instantly accessible.

Shu Yamamoto

picture on the left side, and the corresponding recipe on the right side. No more losing the picture and wondering why you ever saved the recipe in the first place. (You saved it because it looked delicious in the picture, remember?) Use index dividers (also available at the stationery store) to divide your categories. You now have your own customized cookbook that can be expanded or weeded out at any time and can also be kept clean. It's simple to add recipes to the proper category, and if you wish, you can snap one of the sheet-protected recipes out of the binder and work from that one easy-to-clean page, thus eliminating the need to have the bulky books on the counter while you are cooking. If your collection is extensive, you might want to have separate binders for different categories. Any way you look at it, this book takes care of all of your recipes, whether they are on scraps of paper or an entire magazine page. No more recopying by hand onto those stupid little index cards (that always get lost anyway) or shoving clippings into boxes and drawers. With this book, it will be a snap to hone your culinary talents, and they will be remembered with pleasure by all who are lucky enough to taste the results of your last recipe test. Everyone will be asking *you* for your wonderful recipe, which you can keep secret in your personal cookbook or easily share by flipping to the correct page in the book and pulling it out for photocopying.

Rent. File any information you may have regarding your rent, including payments, and your lease in a file marked, simply, Rent. If you have a Financial section, file it there; otherwise file it under *R* in your general files.

Reports. Reports help make the paper world go 'round. It starts in grade school with book reports and dogs us throughout life in a variety of sometimes-veiled ways. "Could you get back to me on that?" queries the boss. A memo reporting on "that" is painstakingly written in response. "I want that report on my desk by ten sharp Monday morning" guarantees a forty-hour report weekend so that you can generate the required bazillion page report. Requiring status reports on a regular basis is management's way of checking up on you. If you are part of the management team these can be good (if you can read past the bluffing and fluffing); if you are an employee, they're a pain in the you-know-what, taking up valuable time that could, after all, be spent doing something else — like working, for example. Financial reports, committee reports, and sales reports all serve some purpose, however obscure, and since the world of reporting is probably here to stay, the best you can do is to resign yourself to the fact that you will either be giving or getting reports sometime in your life. If you're lucky, it won't be every day or every week, but even if you have to deal with them that often, you can probably simplify the whole process a bit with just a few practical principles:

First, if you have to write these things on a regular basis, consider drawing up a boiler plate report that might, for instance, provide an opening statement with a fill-in-the-blanks kind of format:

The sales department had a sales quota for the month of January.

_____

As of the week ending _____, the total sales have reached

_____

You might also choose to list within your report the necessary information requirements (also with a fill in the blanks format):

Month	Quota	Week Ending	Actual Total Sales
_____	_____	_____	_____
_____	_____	_____	_____
_____	_____	_____	_____
_____	_____	_____	_____

You can even use the traditional who, what, where, and when format to outline your report:

Date:	January 1, 1990	(When)
Principals:	Mr. Arnold & Mr. Charles	(Who)
Re:	Meeting in Salt Lake City	(Where)
	to discuss legal proceedings against	
	the ABC Corporation	(What)

You might want to add some or all of these sections to the report (which could be filled in appropriately every time you write a report in the future):

Objective

Description of Services Performed

Discussion

Potential Problem Areas

Conclusion

Final Recommendations

By completing the pertinent sections concisely, you will more than likely answer any of the questions that the powers that be might have and cover your you-know-what at the same time. And the beauty of it is that you don't have to be an accomplished writer to do the report and get your point across. Establishing a format for your reports can save you the enormous amounts of time that it would otherwise take to dream up and put this stuff into coherent language in a report. It also gets right to the point and makes reading the report much simpler.

If you receive reports and your job is to read them, you should insist on this to-the-point format. Otherwise, somebody is probably bamboozling you with pages and pages of poppycock that looks good but means nothing. It takes forever to read the things, so half the time you don't. Which is smart, because there's nothing worth reading in the first place in most of these works of reporting art. So insist on a standard format for all reports, and however it is currently done, tell everyone to reduce the amount of paper they use for their reports by at least 25 percent. Twenty-five percent of what they've been giving you is fiction not fact anyway, so this will help cut that unnecessary information out of the report.

Reports can be filed if they actually say something, and if they are only a page or two or three. If they are massive tomes, however, you should file the things on the bookcase, since storing them in the filing cabinet can be an inefficient use of that space. Instead, file a two- or three-page synopsis of the report in the file and stick the report on a bookcase or in a cabinet for reference if necessary. They can be stored upright like a book in magazine holders on any shelf. (If you wrote the report, you should write the synopsis; if the report came from someone else, and you have the power to do so, request that they also provide you with a synopsis. Otherwise, it may very well be worth your time to dictate some notes regarding your overall impression/synopsis of the report and have them typed and placed in a file for you.) Go through these at least once a year and either throw some of them away (particularly if they are no longer relevant), store them, or cast about to see who else in the office might need to feel important. People who need to feel important love to have bulky reports lying about to serve as a backdrop to and confirmation of their importance. They'll take these things from you, and if anyone ever needs to look at them (unlikely), just send them down to Joe's office; they can go down there and make him feel even more important by asking for and/or about that particular report.

Research. If you need to keep research information, you may need to set up some method of accommodating all of the attendant paperwork. But don't do it unless you have to; remember that there is a wonderful system of libraries to help you research virtually anything you need for special projects. But if, for example, you are a writer, and you need to develop and have on hand lots of research for a current project or for potential projects (watch out for that "potential"—it can get out of hand and become a dumping ground), you may need to have some research files.

Throwing research material into files can keep the paperwork contained, but it is not necessarily the best storage method when you need to access the material in an efficient manner. Rather than files, you may want to make up a research library for yourself utilizing binders. If, for example, you collect historical information, you might want to set up binders for different periods. You might have a binder for each decade or each century, depending on how much research information you are collecting and how you are accumulating it. Then the binders provide "books" of information for you to turn to for reference.

You can set up a filing cabinet or drawer for these research files. Research would be your major category, and you could break the files down by subcategory:

Research — History
        Roman Empire

Research files, as I've said, can get away from you if you're not careful. Periodically stop and look at your motives for clipping something for these files. Will you really use it? If so, when? And how often? Could you, if you had to, get this information from another source, such as the library? If you can, and if you know deep in your heart of hearts that you probably won't look at this material again for months or years, don't file it. Throw it away, and let the librarians provide the (expensive) storage space for this information, rather than doing it yourself. If you have to visit a library once or twice this coming year, you'll actually be the better for it. Libraries are organized, peaceful, and interesting. Which is probably more than can be said about your research files.

Resources. If you keep a great deal of resource information, you may want to set up resource files to hold it. But before you do that, ask yourself how often you are going to actually refer to that paperwork. Because nine times out of ten, people set up resource files primarily because they are compulsive clippers. They clip this and they clip that, sure that they will "need it someday." Then the stuff is crammed into files and never looked at again. (See Articles for more on this.) So if you really only need to make use of some local resources, you could set up one file in your general files and call it either Resources or Local Information. If you want something a bit more concise, you can either set up a small separate Rolodex for just your resources or include them with your other phone numbers and addresses on your (ideally, large) Rolodex. You may want to put the resources on colored Rolodex cards, so that they stand out, or you could put all of the resource information under R — Resources on the Rolodex. Or you can integrate the information and make use of a cross-referencing system to help ensure that you can find the right resource when you need it. For instance, you might want to have a Rolodex card under Plumbers for Acme Plumbing, and you might also want to put the information under Acme Plumbing. That way, you're sure to find it whether you think of it as Acme or Plumbing.

However you choose to organize your resources, as with everything, don't overdo it. Remember, life is sometimes a lot simpler when you let your fingers do the walking through the Yellow Pages for your resource information. Keep only the resources you actually use and a reasonable selection of resources that you might someday use, and after that the business of resources really is best left to libraries and telephone companies.

Resumes. Keep your resumes in a file labeled Resumes, and make sure you check them over at least once each year to see if the information is current and worded properly, given your present working situation. If you regularly review other people's resumes for hiring purposes, keep only those that represent qualified candidates. There is absolutely no reason to keep resumes from qualified clerks if you are searching for a qualified manager. Toss the resumes that don't pass muster; note the date of the receipt and any interview comments you may have on the rest. After you've hired your candidate, keep the other resumes of qualified people for no more than six months to a year. They will have gone on to bigger and better things by then, and you and the company will probably be interested in a totally different type of person for a different position altogether.

Retirement Records. If you want to keep records pertaining to your retirement segregated under the subhead Retirement, simply set up a subcategory in your Financial section. You could then have files such as:

Financial — Retirement
                Pension Plan

Financial — Retirement
                Social Security

If you don't feel like you need this extra subcategory, just file the records alphabetically (in this case under *P* for pension plan, or *S* for Social Security). If you don't have a Financial section, simply integrate them alphabetically in your General files.

Sales Materials. If you work with a lot of sales brochures, data and information sheets, price sheets, and product release sheets, you probably need to evaluate how these many different pieces of paper are being used and stored on a daily basis. Weed out the outdated materials, and get rid of sales pieces that you really never use. If you have pieces that you don't use but that you want to keep because you might need to reuse some of the information on another sales piece, just keep a sample of the piece (file it). One will do; you don't need to keep a truckload.

Organize the materials that are left by grouping all of the like pieces together. Depending on how many different pieces you have, you can store them in a layered wall-mounted rack or in a rolling cart (using file folders in hanging files), or you can purchase square storage units with slots for dozens of different pieces. Check your office supply and furnishings cata-

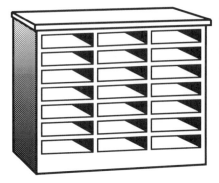

If you regularly use and store sales materials, press materials, study aids, or other handouts, an organizer like this one will organize your materials in one unit, yet keep the individual papers separate. That way it's easy to select exactly what you need for any given occasion.

JBL Graphics, Montrose, California

logue to find what will work best for you, but whichever storage method you use, you will want to store the materials either alphabetically or by the order in which you usually package the pieces. For instance, if you use five different pieces to assemble a special sales package for prospects, you might want to put these five pieces in order, one after the other, in your rack or cart. As you need to assemble new packages or pull out specific sales sheets, all you need to do is to pull it from the proper slot or hanging file, rather than rummage through piles of assorted papers and brochures. To make it even easier, place your rack, storage center, or rolling cart either next to or behind your desk. This way, you won't even have to get out of your chair to pull sales material and get it off ASAP to that hot prospect. And the next time you are on your way to an important sales call, you can grab just what you need on your way out the door.

Continue to monitor your sales materials, discarding those that have been replaced with more up-to-date information. If you work with packages of several pieces, you can assemble those packages in advance and store them in a cart to save time and to keep things organized in a ready-to-go fashion. Keep only what you use, and then use what you have. Go get 'em, tiger!

Sales Prospect Records. A salesperson accumulates sales leads so that those leads can be turned into *sales*. This system often breaks down in the process somewhere between the lead and the actual sale, usually for a very simple reason: The papers are in a pile, and nobody followed up the lead or the prospect. To gain total control over all of your leads, turn them efficiently into qualified prospects, and then follow up to make a sale, the most effective paper management tool you can use is to make yourself a Sales Prospect binder. Here's how to put it together:

SALES PROSPECT

Company

Phone

Contact

Address

Date Contact Comments F/U

Additional Comments

Use this binder to set up a daily follow-up tickler system for all of your prospects. If your prospect needs to be phoned in a future month, put the prospect sheet behind that month. Use the alphabetical tabs to file any notes or paperwork that you need to keep handy for reference when you call your prospect.

JBL Graphics, Montrose, California

Purchase a large three-ring binder at the stationery store. You'll also want to pick up the following sets of dividers that will fit into the binder:

One set of dividers numbered 1 through 31

One set of dividers marked with the months of the year

One set of alphabetical dividers

In the very front of the binder put at least twenty prospect information sheets. You can make your own sheet on a typewriter. Provide space for the following information about your prospect:

Name of Company   Telephone No.

Contact Name

Address

Then leave space for information that you can note as you contact the client. Allow ample room to record more than a few follow-ups (when to call back), since unless you're the hottest salesperson on earth, not all of your prospects are going to buy on the first call. Include the following:

Date of Call   Contact   Comments   Follow-up

Leave room at the bottom of the page for any additional comments you may want to note regarding your conversation with the prospect. For instance, you may have gleaned interesting information about the prospect that you can bring up again in conversation when you call him back. These notes will help you remember that.

When you get a lead, sit down and make the call. While the phone is ringing, start filling in the company name, phone, contact, and address. As you talk to your prospect, fill in the rest of the sheet. When the conversation is concluded, take the prospect sheet and put it either behind a number or a month tab. Let's say the prospect indicates that you might be more successful if you call back after the 15th of the month. Put that sheet behind 20. Each day, turn to the number tab for that day and make your follow-up calls. On the 20th, you will be automatically reminded to call this particular prospect back. Perhaps the prospect is not ready now, and you need to call them back in two months when their budget is up for review. Simply place their prospect sheet behind that monthly tab. On the first of each month, check the follow-up prospects in that section of your binder. Pull the sheets and distribute them among your 1 through 31 daily tabs. Now you will be sure to handle all of your follow-ups throughout the month, without anyone falling through the cracks.

Finally, if you receive any written correspondence from your prospects or if you send out a letter or some pertinent information, you may want to keep a copy of that correspondence in the back of the book, filed alphabetically under the prospect's or the firm's name. As you talk to the prospect it is easy to flip to that correspondence and refer to it. (Only put important material there, however; otherwise the binder will quickly become too bulky and, therefore, unusable.)

Only you know how good you are. Your prospect binder and the information sheets will let you know when to give up and go on to other potential prospects. As you work with the prospect information sheets, and after you have noted several follow-ups with no results, it may be time to retire that prospect so that you can go on to greener pastures. When this happens, pull the prospect sheet and either toss it or, if you must, temporarily file it in archival binders that are set up alphabetically and are stored in a cabinet or closet. If the prospect ever does come in, you can resurrect the information sheet to work with. Once a year throw the old, retired prospect sheets away. By then you will have gone on to develop prospects aplenty into what they were always meant to be—*your sales.*

Schedules. Schedules turn into a paper problem when one person starts juggling several of them at one time. There are travel schedules, baby

SALES PROSPECT

COMPANY: _____ PHONE: _____

CONTACT: _____

ADDRESS: _____

DATE	CONTACT	COMMENTS	F/U DATE

ADDITIONAL COMMENTS:

_____

_____

_____

_____

_____

_____

_____

_____

_____

_____

_____

_____

Use this prospect page to keep track of pertinent information and follow-up dates for each of your important sales prospects.

JBL Graphics, Montrose, California

schedules, meal schedules, school schedules, and entertainment schedules. If you've got kids, they have schedules that impact your schedule. Soon you find yourself searching for the paper with your travel itinerary on it and wondering what happened to that piece of paper that had the Little League schedule on it, so you can figure out if you can be in two places at once. To simplify things and reduce the number of papers involved when more than one schedule is juggled, your best bet is to make a master calendar.

For a busy family, particularly, this can be a lifesaver. Post a very large calendar on the wall; then train each member who is old enough to check his or her own schedule and to mark it on the family schedule. Once a week, a family planning/scheduling powwow should be held to make sure that everybody's gears are going to mesh on the upcoming week's schedule. As the children get older, you'll need to tighten up on the rules. If they forget to consult the schedule or forget to pencil their needs in (and make sure it doesn't conflict with other plans already noted on the calendar), well then, it just might be that Mother's Car and Van Service will *not* be available at a moment's notice to taxi them to their desired destination. Work as a family to teach everyone to respect the other person's time and to resist the temptation to overbook time—theirs or anyone else's.

Likewise, at the office, all of your scheduling should be on or near only one calendar. Make sure it is roomy enough to make notations. Put pieces of paper with special travel directions or itineraries under or in the back of the calendar. When the date rolls around to drive to your appointment or to travel a long distance, your directions are right there for you to take with you. If you have a secretary, let him or her manage your calendar, or at least keep your calendar on your desk so that he or she can check it for information or to add information for you when you are out.

Working with one schedule tells you at a glance when you are overdoing it and heading for a severe time management crisis. It also eliminates all of those superfluous pieces of paper that tend to float around with bits and pieces of your schedule on them. When the year is over, it provides one complete record of where and how you spent your time, and it can be stored as is with your other tax records. If how you spend your time is not tax deductible, you don't even need to keep this calendar. Pitch it and set up your next master calendar so that you can work with *one* schedule and a minimum of attendant paperwork in the upcoming year.

Special Projects. Special projects often generate vast quantities of paper as a by-product. For example, you may be writing a book that requires research in several areas. To keep your papers organized, you would want

You can use the top of your credenza or the top of a folding table to serve as temporary storage for papers and files that you are currently working on in connection with a special project. Make sure the credenza or table is within reach of your desk or work area so that you can get whatever you need instantly.

JBL Graphics, Montrose, California

to make up files for different categories of research, as well as files for your notes and drafts. You would be working on these materials on an ongoing basis, so you wouldn't want to integrate these project files into your permanent files just yet. Other project file examples include lawsuits, special university projects, fundraising events, and major deals involving negotiation with several people.

Assuming you are not accumulating all of this paper just for the sake of collecting it or because you can't quite figure out what to do with it, you will need to set up some special project files. A rolling cart is perfect for the temporary storage of these files (you can hang them in hanging folders in the top of the cart). Often these carts have baskets under the files that provide extra space for supplies that might go with the project (such as reference magazines or stationery). A spare surface is also handy for those times when you might need to sort and reorganize or hold some of the project materials. This surface can be your credenza top, a "project table" (either a portable table that you can put up as needed or a table that is a fixed piece of furniture in the room), or it can be the bed that is in the spare bedroom where your desk is located.

You won't need to write the word, "project" on these files, since the fact that you have it stored in the project cart will tell you that it is a project you are currently working on. When you are finished with the project, simply integrate the files into your permanent filing system or store them in transfile boxes. Be careful not to automatically store projects just because you want to remind yourself of how hard you worked. Once a project is completed, keep only what is legally or financially necessary. Throw the rest away.

Stocks and Bonds. File these in a safety deposit box or a fireproof strong-box or filing cabinet. For more on how to file the attendant paperwork, see Investments.

Subscriptions. Subscriptions to magazines, newspapers, and trade journals can pose two problems. The first is the amount of extra paper it brings into the house or office. It's not enough to deal with all the other paperwork in your life, now you've got all this *reading* to do as well. If your subscriptions are apparent by the stacks and piles of magazines and newspapers that are starting to take over, read Magazines and Newspapers for some tips on how to get a handle on all of those piles.

The second problem generated by subscriptions is posed when you try to keep track of what is paid and what is not. What should be a simple bookkeeping function (write a check, and it's paid) becomes very complicated when each magazine, newspaper, and journal vendor adds to the confusion by sending you renewal notices promising special deals six months before your current subscription is due to run out. You sign up because it sounds like a bargain, but in the back of your mind is this nagging thought that you just paid for a subscription for this particular paper or magazine. Half the time, you're right. You did pay, and I think it's a trick or at least a plot to keep us all so confused that from time to time we pay twice what we're supposed to by double-paying the bill during the year, totally cancelling out any benefits we might have received from their "special deal." It goes almost without saying that the first thing you should do is review your subscriptions and resolve *not* to renew those that are no longer of any interest to you. Renewing subscriptions is something of a knee-jerk reaction that repeats itself mindlessly year after year. Now is the time to take a good look at your subscriptions. If you have magazines you've outgrown or are bored with, or if you get three newspapers a day and only have time to read two, get rid of some of those excess subscriptions. Try to avoid that temptation to pick up other subscriptions for different periodicals, unless you are sure you'll be captivated by each and every issue.

Next, set up a file marked Subscriptions. You can put this in your Financial files if you have them, or you can file it alphabetically in the general files. Every time you renew a subscription, make sure that you mark the date paid, along with the check number and the amount of the check on your portion of the payment stub. If the periodical has not provided a payment stub for you to keep for your records (I happen to think this is a deliberate trick to add to our confusion), just make a small note showing the name of the periodical, the amount and the date paid, the term of the subscription you are paying for (i.e., twelve months, twenty-four months, etc.), and the check number; file this note in your Subscriptions file.

Now, before you renew any subscriptions in the future, first check your file to see when you last renewed for that particular periodical. If it looks like they are trying to get you to renew just a few months after your last payment, ignore the renewal notice. (Throw it away—don't keep it; it's too confusing.) They won't forget one of their favorite subscribers—you. They'll keep sending you those "bargain" renewal notices right up until your subscription runs out and for at least a month or two after it has expired.

When you drop a subscription, remove any paperwork from the file and toss it unless you need to keep it for tax purposes (here, generally your cancelled check is all you need). If, in spite of this simple system, your subscriptions start to get away from you again, you could give yourself a fabulous gift of time and some money to go along with it. All you have to do is ignore them all; don't renew a single one. You'll have time and money to burn once you mark your mailbox, desk, and front porch "off limits" to subscriptions. You wanna read a newspaper? Pick it up on the way to work and read it when you're goldbricking during the day. For magazines, you can always grab one and read the best parts while you are standing in line at the supermarket or waiting in the doctor's office. Or you can get one at the airport on your way out of town. This approach to subscriptions is radical, but it works. Think about it. If you let them *all* go, by the end of the year you will have saved yourself the trouble of shuffling *hundreds* of pounds of *paper!*

Tax Records. Tax records obviously need to be kept in good order just in case that great Tax Collector in the sky decides to come after you. How people keep their tax records varies widely. Some people think "tax records" means every receipt and piece of paper that they happen upon that might be included in the deductions on their tax return. Some people think "tax records" means tax returns and maybe end-of-year W-2 forms and the like. Both groups are right, of course; it's all meaningful paperwork that has dramatic financial and legal implications for the taxpayer. Looking at all of the pertinent paperwork, start by *not* doing the following:

1. Putting all of your receipts and related tax paperwork into a drawer, bag, box, or humongous manila envelope that says, Taxes.

2. Throwing away a lot of your paperwork because, after all, your check is your receipt.

Stuffing everything into some deadly concealed pile only postpones the day of reckoning. Before you file your return you or somebody else will have to go through and sort this mess. Since it represents such a dreaded chore, chances are you'll wait until the last minute to do it, driving yourself and your accountant crazy in the process. Conversely, tossing financial records because you have cancelled checks is probably all right in some cases, but there are times when the IRS may want to see the receipt for a series of purchases to clarify exactly *what* was purchased. Don't be so hasty here; keep these filed throughout the year, and store them and destroy them on a retention schedule that your accountant says will work for your tax circumstances.

For all of these tax deductible papers, the best solution is to file them throughout the year in an organized manner. When the year is concluded, simply pull the files, tall the financial information from each well-organized file, and move it to storage. All you have to do then is make up a few new manila folders for the new year and drop them into the already existing hanging file folder in your filing drawer or cabinet. Additionally, by keeping your deductible financial papers in order as you go along, you will have no problem resolving any problems that might arise during the year regarding any payments you may have made or are due to make. Simply go to the proper file. No need to dig through stacks of cancelled checks (this is a last resort as proof of payment) or rummaging through rowdy piles of receipts.

Once you have decided to keep your expenses and other tax-related paperwork filed properly throughout the year, the only other files to set up are those for the tax returns themselves. You may also want one back-up file for each year that can hold W-2 forms and interest income statements that you receive at year's end for filing purposes. This is also a good place to keep your written calculations if you do your own return. Then, if there is ever a question about how you arrived at a certain figure, you can refer back to your notes. Title this back-up file Tax Back-up and include the year on the title.

After that, make a file for your tax returns. If your tax circumstances are simple and you have a basic federal and state return with no deductions to speak of, one file marked Tax Returns and the year will do. If you have more complicated returns, or if you have several returns each year, make a file for each type of return. Here are some examples, using the year 1990:

Tax Returns — Corporate 1990

Tax Returns — Personal 1990

Tax Returns — Quarterly Estimated 1990

You may even want to go further if you are involved in a business that requires filing all types of returns for employees and other matters. You can add further definition to your files by setting up files for the Schedules that you file. For example:

Tax Returns — Schedule A 1990

Tax Returns — Schedule B 1990

Tax Returns — Schedule C 1990

When you pull your Back-up file and your other expense files for computation at tax time, you might want to put some of the more pertinent schedule related records into the Schedule files rather than in the Back-up file.

Tax returns should be kept for at least several years. But there is no need to keep more than one or two years' worth in your current filing system; anything prior to that can be moved to storage with your archival files. Check with the IRS or with your tax preparer on the length of time you are required to keep these records. In the meantime, remember that an ounce of prevention is worth a pound of cure. Keep these records sensibly organized, and if you are ever faced with an audit, it will be easier to deal with. It still won't be pleasant, of course, but at least your paperwork will be in order.

Telephone. I have a great deal to say about today's telephone system. I was once a long-distance operator, back in those old-timey days when operators had jillions of wires that they plugged into a board as they actually said, "May I help you?" When I heard about direct dialing, I balked in a major way (ZIP codes provoked the same response, and now I'm up in arms about pumping your own gas). It seems like the telephone company tells you things are going to be simpler — and in some ways they are — but in too many other ways the system has become a confusing morass. Buying, operating, and repairing equipment is a real head scratcher, so you've got to keep paperwork on the kind of equipment and any warranty that applies. The bill is a joke; I once tried to figure out just the *surcharges,* and it sent me into a mathematical coma. Most people do what I do, they pay up and, for the most part, shut up. Otherwise you could drive yourself looney trying to justify the charges and the calculations on the bill. And as for the service that the operators provide these days — that is, if you can figure out what number to dial to actually get one on the line — well, I won't even go into that. This book is about paper, not social injustice.

So, to keep your end of the telephone paperwork cycle as simple as possible, keep your telephone bills in a file titled Telephone. You can put it in your Financial section or in your general files. You might as well keep any information sheets or brochures that you have about the equipment here as well. When the equipment dies on you and is unfixable, throw these brochures away and replace them with the brochures for the new disposable telephone that you will now have to buy. Once a year weed out your telephone bills. Unless they are tax deductible, throw the suckers away. You've got another year of undecipherable telephone bills to look forward to; no need to keep living in the past.

Tickets. Tickets beg to get lost in the paper shuffle. Traffic tickets, lottery tickets, raffle tickets, airline tickets, and tickets to sporting and entertainment events all tend to mix and mingle with other receipts, mail and assorted paperwork. Just when you need to grab them, they've mysteriously disappeared. When this happens, bad things can occur. If you lose a ticket to an event, your spouse or other guest could very well throw a conniption fit. Lost raffle or lottery tickets can mean the pot of gold that got away. And we all know that having "lost" traffic tickets is just no excuse for not paying them; once you haven't paid a few of them, guess what: You may get to go to jail. (Do not pass Go.) And if you lose your plane, train, or bus tickets, you can be *stranded.* (For more on these tickets, see Travel.)

To take care of your tickets, first put raffle, lottery, or tickets to events in a box or basket. Call this the "ticket basket." Don't allow anything else to be put in there, and you'll always be ready to take your tickets with you to the ball game or to collect your lottery or raffle winnings.

Traffic tickets are another matter. When these come in or appear pasted on your car's windshield, *do not ignore them!* Put them in your To Pay file or basket immediately. These are bills that need to be paid, the sooner the better. To ignore these is to court disaster. (In my book, *How to Get Organized When You Don't Have the Time,* I have a chapter on "Procrastination" that recalls a traffic ticket dilemma that turned into an expensive set of consequences for one poor sap who ignored his traffic tickets. Trust me; you don't want this to happen to you.) So pay these "bills." When you pay them, make sure that you note the traffic ticket number on your check and check stub. It helps to copy the ticket as well and put it in a file titled Traffic Tickets. I say this only because my experience has been that the computerized bureaucracy of the motor vehicles department can easily become a monster out to get you. I read about one such giant agency that had screwed up royally. Their computers had somehow mixed up or lost all information pertaining to who had paid which traffic tickets. So they just billed everybody all over again and, I guess, hoped that no one noticed their little, er, mistake. And you know what, if you hadn't written that ticket number on your check and copied the ticket for your files, you would have to pay again. Because fighting the motor vehicles department is worse than trying to fight city hall. With or without (paper) documentation to back up your case, it's going to give you a nervous breakdown. And all because you lost a stupid *ticket.*

To Do Lists. (See also Notes.) If you've got more than one to do list, you have too many. Some people make to do lists all over the place and then spend twenty minutes every day reorganizing and rewriting all of their lists. No wonder they never get anything done — they're too busy organizing the lists! Don't keep old, expired to do lists. And only keep one to do list for the here and now. You should keep it in a datebook that you carry, or if you don't want to do that, assign one small notepad for that purpose. Don't let yourself start writing other notes about other things on your to do list. Cross things off as you do them. Rewrite the list a couple of times a week. And whatever you do, use the KISS rule: Keep It Simple, Stupid.

Travel. The travel files very often become the dumping ground for dreams. Articles about faraway places are clipped, dreamed about, and added to the Travel file. Brochures are perused and dropped into the file. Along with these fantasies, used plane tickets, boarding passes, travel expenses, and frequent flyer information are dumped into the file. Before long it becomes the world's most outdated mess. So what do you do? You leave it as is and *start another file!*

Instead of resorting to this, why not deal with your current and future messes by setting up three files:

Travel — Expenses

Travel — Frequent Flyer

Travel — Information

Drop expense receipts and information into the Expenses file. Your used tickets can go here as well, although if you paid by check or credit card, you probably don't have to keep them. At the end of the year, tabulate any tax-deductible expenses for your return and move the receipts to storage, leaving the Expense file set up for the coming year.

Your frequent flyer information should go in the Frequent Flyer file. Do not file the brochures and other miscellaneous junk mail that the carriers send you with your frequent flyer updates. All you need is the paperwork that explains your benefits and the statements that show your mileage accrual. If you maintain accounts with more than one airline, you will want to make separate files, since it is much easier to keep on top of your mileage statistics if you do it by airline. For example:

Travel—Frequent Flyer
     American Airlines

Travel—Frequent Flyer
     Delta

If you find that any one airline is slow to send you regular statements or updates reflecting your most recent accrual, you may want to keep your used plane tickets and boarding passes in the appropriate frequent flyer file. That way, you can compare the tickets against the statements to make sure that your account has been credited properly. Once you have taken advantage of your accumulated points and used them, you can throw away the old statements. Keep only the new accrual statements for future use of your frequent flyer points.

    Travel—Information is where you can dump all of those travel dreams. If you are a compulsive travel clipper, you may find that you stuff this file folder full almost immediately. If this is the case, I suggest that you stop automatically saving and clipping everything that you ever dreamed about in travel terms. Next, you might want to divide your Travel—Information file a bit more by setting up some regional files. For instance:

Travel—Information
     Asia

Travel—Information
     Europe

Travel—Information
     United States

Clean these files out at least once or twice each year. Much of this information becomes outdated and can be eliminated. With some of the rest of these papers and brochures, a good dose of reality will do the elimination trick. Are you ever really going to Bora Bora? Will you ever buy that RV to travel the backroads of America? Get rid of stuff that pertains to travel that you know you will not be able to take in the coming year. The world will not come to an end. Even if you decided to plan a special trip next year and found you had thrown away the information that you had been accumulating, you'd have no problem getting a truckload of information from travel agents and the library.

The last type of potential travel paperwork concerns plane or train ticket(s) and your itinerary. If you travel regularly for business, you may want to set up a file folder and place it in the front of your desk file drawer or in a hot file next to your desk. Title the file Travel—Trips and add the trip destination. If you have several trips coming up in the next several weeks, you would make several files. For example:

Travel—Trips
Chicago

Travel—Trips
Los Angeles

Travel—Trips
New York

Then, as tickets and itineraries are issued, they can be dropped into this file. You may also want to put other important information regarding the trip into the file, such as notes about appointments you may have or additional materials (such as sales materials) you will need to put together to take with you. When you are ready to leave, pull the file, check it to see if there is anything else you need to do, and take it, the tickets, and the itinerary with you. Don't forget to mark your working calendar with your travel plans as they are made and confirmed, so that you and everyone around you are kept posted on your availability and whereabouts.
Happy trails!

Utilities. Utility bills, including gas, water, and power, can all be filed in a file titled Utilities. If you want to break them down, you can categorize them:

Utilities—Electricity

Utilities—Gas

Utilities—Water

Generally, however, this is not necessary, since the bills are usually small single sheets of paper, and since people rarely go back to challenge a bill.

Pick any method you wish for storing them (you could even combine two types of utilities in one file if you like, such as Utilities — Gas and Electric), and keep your bills for one year. At tax time, unless the bills are deductible, throw last year's bills away.

Vendors. If you are in a business that regularly deals with a large number of vendors or suppliers, you may want to set up a separate filing drawer to keep those records, assigning at least one file to all of your major vendors. You can keep product information in this file along with price lists for products. You may also want to set up an Accounts Payable file for vendors that you do business with on a very regular basis. These invoices from the vendors can be put in this file under the vendor's company name in the Vendor drawer, or you can put vendor invoices into your Accounts Payable files, if you have set up your Financial files to include such a section (see Accounts Payable). Or you can set up an Accounts Payable file that is loosely organized by vendor. For instance:

Financial — Accounts Payable
Vendors — A-G

Financial — Accounts Payable
Vendors — H-P

Financial — Accounts Payable
Vendors — R-Z

This works well if you deal with several vendors but do not have enough invoice paperwork to set up a separate file for each vendor. For major vendors with lots of monthly activity, you would want to keep one file for each area of paper activity:

Vendor — Hanson Company
Accounts Payable

Vendor — Hanson Company
Correspondence

Vendor — Hanson Company
Product Information

In the above example, you can file the files under Vendor, or you can file the files alphabetically first under *H* for Hanson (leaving off the Vendor title), or you can reverse the information on the file title and integrate the files by function rather than company into your files:

Accounts Payable— Hanson Company	(filed under *A*) Subcategory H
Correspondence— Hanson Company	(filed under *C*) Subcategory H
Product Information— Hanson Company	(filed under *P*) Subcategory H

How you set up your vendor files will depend entirely on how much activity and how many vendors you have. You may even just want to keep one Miscellaneous file for vendors if your contact with vendors is minimal. However you handle it, clean out the files once each year to get rid of outdated product information and price sheets and move accounts payable information to storage for tax back-up purposes.

Warranties and Instructions. This is the file where you stuff those obnoxious warranties and instructions for appliances and electronic equipment that you purchase. One file should handle all of this paperwork so long as you take care to not automatically throw all of the important looking information that comes with your new products into the file. Take an extra minute or two when you unpack the product to go through the cards and paperwork that comes with your new goodie. Only file important warranty information, and before you file it, make a note of the expiration date on the card or paper. When you clean out the file (at least once a year) quickly scan the expiration dates on the warranties and throw away anything that has expired. You can also keep instructions to equipment in this file, but you do have some other options that can save you filing cabinet space (these instruction booklets take up a lot of space in the file). You can put the instructions near their point of use. For example, instead of filing the instructions, you can put the VCR instructions *under* the VCR, the telephone answering machine instructions *under* the answering machine, the food processor instructions in the kitchen drawer *nearest* the food processor, and so on. That way, when you need to refer to instructions, you won't have to dig through an overstuffed file to find it. Other instructions can be tossed after they are read. If you have instructions on how to assemble the electric toothbrush stand, and you have assembled it successfully, you can throw the assembly instructions away. After all, you're not planning to disassemble the thing for any reason, so why keep those pieces of paper?

Finally, it goes without saying that if you replace something with another, newer product, get rid of the paperwork that is in the file for the old product at the time that you file the paperwork for the new product. That way, your Warranties and Instructions file will be functional and up to date at all times.

Will. You can make a file titled Will for this document, or you can keep it in a safety deposit box. Make sure that someone (perhaps your lawyer as well as a trusted friend or relative) knows about your will and your wishes regarding the execution of it (for more on this see The Master File). And if you want the terms of your will to be a big surprise to everybody, probably the best way to go is to keep it in your safety deposit box, with a copy at your lawyer's office.

Sadly, this is one piece of paper many people procrastinate about getting. If you have any assets at all, you owe it to yourself and to the people or charities that you care about to make a will. For this is one piece of paper that executes your wishes after you are gone, whether you go tomorrow or forty years from now.

PART THREE

KEEPING PAPER
IN ITS PLACE

TWELVE STEPS TO LIFELONG PAPER MANAGEMENT

Once you've organized all of your papers, you can follow these twelve steps into the future, so that your papers never back up on you again:

1. *Open Your Mail.* Open and sort the mail as soon as you get it. Throw away all junk inserts, then sort the mail into four categories: To Do, To Pay, To Read, and To File. Junk the junk mail immediately.

2. *Work to Overcome Information Anxiety.* Stop thinking that you have to be totally informed and aware. Limit the amount of information you try to absorb, and stop feeling guilty about that information that is beyond your limits.

3. *Be Realistic about Your Reading.* Evaluate your subscription list on a regular basis. If you find yourself falling behind in your reading, let some of those subscriptions go. Have someone prescreen some of your business-related reading if you can, and do some screening yourself by clipping only the most important articles for reading and throwing the rest of the periodical away.

4. *Decide to Decide.* Make a commitment to making decisions about your paperwork. Stop putting papers in piles "just for now" because you can't make a decision about what to do with them. Decide to read it, file it, pay it, or do it. Then *do it.*

5. *Prioritize.* To ensure that you don't let your To Do box turn into a burial ground, start each day by going through the box and prioritizing what needs to be done. Move these papers to a priority position in the center of your desk. Then deal with those papers first.

6. *Quit Procrastinating.* Procrastination is often the beginning of the end. If you find yourself procrastinating on your paperwork, try to do the worst first. Or tackle it in small segments—inch by inch it's a cinch. Or, better yet, delegate it. Let somebody else take care of it for you.

7. *Stop Being a Copycat.* Resist the urge to copy everything you have on paper. Every time you copy something on a duplicating machine, you're contributing to the blizzard of papers blanketing the human race.

8. *Stop Dumping.* Quit using your files as a dumping ground. Remember that 80 percent of everything you file you will never look at again.

9. *Use the KISS Rule.* Resist the urge to give in to your perfectionist

tendencies by setting up complicated filing systems. Use the KISS rule—Keep It Simple, Stupid.

10. *Learn to Let Go.* Be selective about the papers you keep, particularly where mementos are concerned. Choose a special sampling of paper memories and let the rest of your paper past go.

11. *Purge Your Papers Regularly.* Make it a rule to purge your files and papers at least once each year and more often if possible. When you have a file out, clean it out.

12. *Daily Duty.* Spend five or ten minutes each day tidying up your work area and prioritizing your paperwork for the next day. The following day will get off to a much better start if your desk is organized and you are not faced with overwhelming piles of paper.

ORGANIZING TIPS FOR PAPER PUSHERS

Use these quick tips every day to keep one step ahead of your piles of paper:

- Set aside some time every day to do your paperwork, and it won't back up on you; make sure you set aside more time than you need, and for best results, pick a time of the day when your energy is high.

- Invest in a good desk, filing cabinet, and any other office and paper storage equipment that you need.

- Never keep work in progress inside desk drawers.

- Don't use the top of your desk as a storage area; it is a work area.

- Stop spreading your papers all over your desk; work on one piece of paper at a time and keep the rest of them neatly organized in a stack on a corner of the desk.

- Don't let your In box be a storage box; think of it as a Move It box, and then make sure you deal with the papers in there and "move" them.

- Use the four-step paper processing system; divide your papers into To Do, To Pay, To Read, and To File.

- Limit yourself to cabinet space for the sake of discipline—remember that storage space costs money.

- Establish a To Go area for papers, mail, and files that you need to take with you when you leave.

- Keep a large trash can near your desk or work area.

- Keep stationery and supplies close at hand.

- Don't use a bulletin board.

- Resist the urge to compulsively make notes on dozens of different pieces of paper and notepads.

- Never have more than one To Do list at any one time.

- Turn your briefcase into a personal organizer by setting up files marked To Do, To Pay, To Read and To File. Keep a supply of stationery, postage, and other supplies in your briefcase so you can really work on the road.

- Don't write so many memos.

- Use a letter opener to open your mail.

- Open your mail near a trash can.

- Date stamp papers when they come in the mail so you can effectively prioritize.

- Don't save sales, boring, stupid, or cover letters.

- Call instead of write.

- Get some inexpensive return address stickers and use them on your envelopes if you don't have printed stationery.

- Get your name off of mailing lists.

- Don't order too many subscriptions.

- Don't keep catalogues longer than sixty days.

- Carry postcards with you so you can keep up with your personal correspondence by knocking off a few quick cards when you are kept waiting.

- Keep a small supply of greeting cards handy.

- Spend ten minutes each day to dash off a personal note to someone.

- Send a postcard instead of a letter.

- Don't hang on to every greeting card you receive.

- Set up a message center for phone messages.

- Keep a pen and notepad near the phone.

- Keep call slips contained, and don't keep them forever.

- Keep your phone numbers on a large-wheel Rolodex.

- Keep phone numbers in a container to transfer to a Rolodex later.

- Keep a calendar near your phone and carry one with you as well.

- Make your scheduling decisions immediately and note them on your calendar so you can decide what to do with any related papers or invitations (keep them with your calendar or toss them).

- Mark important dates, such as birthdays and anniversaries, on your calendar in advance, at the beginning of the year.

- Schedule uninterrupted reading time.

- Carry reading with you to read on the run.

- Stop clipping so many articles and cartoons, and get rid of at least 50 percent of the ones you already have.

- Clip magazine articles and throw the rest of the magazine away.

- Keep a stapler and a pair of scissors in your To Read basket.

- Have your secretary preread journals for you to clip only the most important articles for your perusal.

- Throw newspapers away immediately.

- Organize your paid bills as you go; don't just stuff hundreds of invoices and receipts into a box or large envelope.

- Keep your bank statements in the envelope they arrived in; mark the date of the statement, month, and year on the front of the envelopes and store them in a box on a shelf.

- When you travel, keep your receipts in an envelope in your pocket, handbag, or briefcase.

- Recap your expenses once each week and complete your reimbursement request at that time.

- Get rid of outdated rubber stamps and old letterhead.

- Throw out any records that are outdated due to pricing or address information.

- If the IRS says you don't need to keep them, get rid of expired policies and records pertaining to things you no longer own.

- Check with your accountant, attorney, and the IRS to find out how long you need to keep records; date them with an expiration date before they go into storage, and once each year toss all of the files with the expiration date on it.

- Get rid of all of the papers relating to previously completed charity work that has nothing to do with what is going on *now*.

- Don't keep calendars just because you like the pictures.

- Don't keep old travel brochures, and be selective about what you keep from now on.

- Don't keep maps as mementos.

- Just because somebody gives you a business card doesn't mean you have to keep it; throw some of these away.

- Get rid of your college papers.

- Get rid of old recipes that you never use.

- Organize the recipes that you do use into your own custom cookbook.

- Don't be so quick to throw out your financial papers and so slow to throw out your paper mementos.

- Put a two-drawer filing cabinet next to your desk.

- Keep action files near you.

- Establish a working storage area for your current project files.

- Keep a master file for emergencies.

- Only buy full-suspension filing cabinets.

- Use a hanging file system for your files.

- Always put a manila folder inside the hanging folder in your filing cabinet.

- Never remove the hanging file folder from the drawer.

- Don't use accordion files.

- Create as few categories as possible in your filing system and use a simple alphabetical system for filing within those categories.

- Make your file identification labels consistent and easy to understand.

- Don't index your files—it's too complicated and an unnecessary extra step.

- Don't allow yourself to have Pending files.

- Resist the urge to color code your files.

- Don't file junk or bulky items.

- Put the most recent piece of paper on top of the other papers in the file so that the file stays in chronological order.

- Unfold papers before you file them; never put them into the file inside an envelope.

- Alphabetize papers as you go; use an alphabetical sorter.

- Score the bottom of manila and hanging file folders when the file starts to get full.

- Don't overstuff your files.

- Move records that are more than two years old into your archival/storage boxes or cabinets.

- Store bulky items, such as trade journals, on bookcases rather than in the files.

- Keep meeting records organized chronologically in a binder.

- Keep plans and large rolled papers in a small, round trash can or in an architect's bin.

- Keep filing supplies near the filing cabinet, but never in the filing cabinet.

- Don't order more office supplies than you can store.

- Set up a filing system for your children in a rolling cart; once each year select some of their papers as mementos and transfer them to storage boxes.

- Recycle children's art by giving it to grandma or using it for holiday wrapping paper.

- Don't let your fear of letting go get in your way; throw papers away!

- Don't let perfectionism get in the way of delegating paper pushing and filing chores—someone else really can take care of it for you; it may not be perfect, but it will be *done.*

- If you have support staff, make sure they are organized; if their organizational skills are poor, consider replacing them.

- Make sure you invest in a procedure manual for your company or department; then keep it updated as procedures change.

- Don't be afraid to have a professional come in to analyze your paper-pushing methods; they could streamline how your company handles paper and save you time and money.

BUYING GUIDE

One of the first steps in organizing the paper in your life might very well be to make a trip to the office supply store for supplies. This guide will give you some information in advance so that you can be more precise in expressing your needs at the store, thus saving yourself the time and energy required to wander stupidly up and down one aisle after another trying to figure out exactly what it was you were supposed to buy for what purpose. Since helpful clerks always seem to be either nonexistent or in very short supply at most office supply stores, you may just want to make a list to suit your needs from this section of the book, or you can combine it with the shopping checklist that you developed from the checklists in Part One, or you may just want to take this book with you for easy reference right there at the store.

Addresses and Business Cards

Rolodex is your answer for organization of this information. They make several models, but the best one with the most growth potential is the wheel-type Rolodex. In addition to their standard models, they also have a rotary business card file that can keep business card information readily accessible. It comes with transparent plastic sleeves, so it's simple to slip the card into a sleeve in the proper alphabetical order.

Other options include purchasing a punching device (such as the Personal Punch™) to custom fit business cards directly onto your Rolodex. These handheld punches cut notches directly into the business card so that the card can then be placed directly onto the Rolodex tracks. Watch where the cut falls, however, since it might obliterate some critical information that's printed along the bottom of the card. This possibility is eliminated altogether if you purchase and use adhesive-backed prenotched strips by Izer International (available at the office supply store). Simply pull away the strip covering the adhesive and stick the business card on the strip — this makes it instantly ready for the Rolodex. To ensure that the extra piece on the business card doesn't make the cards stand up so high that they block the alphabetical dividers, you can put the dividers on strips as well.

Archival Paper Storage

For storing inactive papers, transfile boxes by Fellowes provide a simple way to store papers in an inactive area, freeing up your filing cabinets for storage of active papers. Transfile boxes can be purchased at the office supply store. These sturdy containers are ready to assemble and can be reused for storage indefinitely or disassembled to store flat when not in use.

Calendars

A good calendar is a must. Today calendars come in all sizes and shapes and can be carried with you or left on the desk or both. Selecting a calendar is a personal decision in many cases. Size and style, along with the functional features available, come into play when choosing a calendar. Some of the best on the market today are Week-at-a-Glance, Ryam, Day Runner, and Quo Vadis. All are available at office supply and stationery stores. One of the best, Day-Timers, is available only by mail from Day-Timers Inc., Allentown, Pennsylvania 18001. Their catalogue is well worth a look before you make your decision.

Daily Paper Flow Organizers

Wire baskets for holding sorted mail (i.e., To Do, To Pay, To Read, To File) are always the best bet for keeping incoming mail and paperwork efficiently sorted. Don't forget to buy a set of posts if you decide to maximize space efficiency by stacking the baskets.

Hot file lucite holders (check with your office supply store for brand name; Eldon is a good possibility) provide extra space for keeping current files nearby. These containers can be mounted on the wall next to your desk or attached with magnets to a metal surface (such as a filing cabinet). With this organizer, you can keep several files within reach and still have your desktop clear for work space.

The Sort-Pal™ paper sorter by Pendaflex is yet another way to keep daily papers organized. This expanding sorter separates copies, letters to sign, and so forth. The sorter includes labeled dividers along with blank labels for your custom headings, and the compact portability of the sorter makes it easy to transport papers, sorted, from place to place. It is ideal for use as a sorter in your briefcase as well.

Desk Organizers

Hunt Manufacturing provides a complete line of desktop organizers and trays. Large metal desktop organizers generally fit across the width of the desk and serve to further define the desk as a workstation area. The different tray combinations on these desk add-ons provide organized fingertip storage for forms, stationery supplies, and routine paperwork that is being routed. Smaller versions of these desktop workstation organizers are also available in metal horizontal and/or vertical trays. These fit nicely on the front corner of the desk and can hold stationery supplies and forms that are used daily. These trays and desktop dividers can add valuable functional storage space to a desk area that otherwise lacks adequate storage space for papers, forms, and supplies used on a daily basis.

Filing Supplies — Binders

There is a wide selection of binders available on the market for your filing, organization, and presentation needs. One of the most serviceable is by View Binder™ from K&M Company. The plastic cover makes the binder easy to customize; simply slip in a page describing the contents on the front of the binder and add an identifying strip on the spine. If the binder is used frequently, the plastic cover makes it easy to clean with a damp rag.

Binder Index Dividers. To organize and divide the contents of your binders, use Aigner® dividers. You can find prestamped dividers that are marked alphabetically, numerically, or by month. You can also buy dividers with tabs and paper inserts so that you can type the title and customize the dividers to suit your needs. Plain index dividers with colored or clear tabs are also available. I like the clear tabs; once the tabs are inserted, I think it is easier to see and read through clear rather than colored plastic.

Sheet Protectors. To keep important papers in binders from getting frayed, put them in plastic sheet protectors. You can buy them in a box of one hundred, or you can purchase only a few at a time. If you don't want to punch holes in the paper that needs to be in the binder, look for letter- or legal-sized sheet protectors that have an *extra* strip with the holes in it along one side to fit into the binder. These protectors are more expensive than standard sheet protectors (where the holes fall within the dimensions of the protected area), but it is well worth the cost to organize and preserve papers without punching holes in them.

Filing Supplies — Labels

Avery makes labels of all types, so it pays to stop at the Avery label rack in the office supply store. If you select their file folder labels with no colored stripe (opting for plain white instead), you won't get caught in the color-coding trap (e.g., you don't have the right colored labels so of course you can't file), and you'll have a bit more typing room on the label itself.

Avery also makes labels specifically for the plastic tabs on hanging file folders. These labels have a special adhesive that sticks directly onto the plastic tab of the hanging folder. If you hate trying to type the strips that go with the hanging file folder plastic tabs, these labels can provide an easy alternative. Once typed, the label can either be applied to the paper insert and slipped into the plastic tabs, or it can be affixed directly onto the front of the plastic tab.

Finally, for labeling binders, get Avery binder labels. These labels use a permanent adhesive that adheres to vinyl binders and notebooks.

Filing Supplies — Folders

Smead® makes a variety of file folders, but the folder that's a must is their third-cut manila file folder, which is best purchased in boxes of one hundred (they'll go much faster than you think). They also make divided classification folders and work with people to fill custom design orders for these folders to suit specific needs. They make pocket file folders and they sell green file folders preprinted with the alphabet to serve as miscellaneous file folders.

Gussco makes some of the best partition classification folders on the market. Made from sturdy pressboard, these Dura-Press™ Partition Folders include fasteners for papers and pockets for loose items such as photos, envelopes, or small documents.

Pendaflex™ is the name to look for in hanging file folders. Available in a variety of colors, the Pendaflex folders fit most file cabinet drawers perfectly (not all hanging folders fit right, and when the fit is wrong, they don't slide smoothly in the drawer). In addition to their standard hanging folders, they have box-bottom files with sides to hold bulky material (such as computer printouts) and ensure that papers do not fall out the side. (This is one case where an interior manila file folder may not be workable due to the bulk of the papers.) *Reminder:* When you buy your hanging files, get clear tabs (they're easier to see) and don't pick exotically colored file folders. The store will tend to stock a common color (such as green) the most, so go with that color. That way, when you need more folders, the office supply store will be certain to have what you need.

Furniture

Office furniture must suit personal tastes and be functional and space efficient. There are hundreds of options available, including the Space Maxim-

You can design your desk or workspace by stretching a hollow core door or a piece of laminated or butcher block wood across a couple of two-drawer filing cabinets.

izer Desk by Litning and the space-saving mobile computer cart from O'Sullivan. These are only two of the many possibilities for computer workstations. Full-suspension filing cabinets by Steelcase or Hon are always good. Desks are a personal choice, but whichever brand you select, make sure it has at least one filing drawer, one drawer for stationery supplies, and one drawer for pens, pencils, and other small items. Don't forget to get a good lamp or swing arm type light to illuminate your immediate work area — whether it's a desk, typing extension, or computer workstation.

Finally, take your time and select a good chair on wheels (for easy maneuverability) that is comfortable and supports your back. You'll be spending a fair amount of your working life in that chair, so make your selection with care and foresight.

Stores that sell office or storage furniture are good places to make these purchases, as are discount office supply warehouses and discount department and building supply stores.

Portable Paper Organizers

Rubbermaid makes several portable paper organizers that are especially suitable for keeping everything organized in the car. Their Auto Office™ Seat Desk System is great for people like sales representatives who operate primarily from their cars. Storage compartments in this unit accommodate hanging files, paper supplies, forms, pens, pencils, maps, and oversized items such as planners, calculators, and dictaphones. It also has a desktop-like surface with a clipboard that swivels into position for writing in the car or that can be removed. The hanging file bin can also be removed and transported easily between home, office, and client.

Other products include portable file bins in different sizes. Some models have compartments for pens, pencils, and clips as well.

Closet Maid makes a rolling cart that can be adapted to hold hanging files in the top and store supplies or pending paperwork requiring attention in the baskets below. Made of white wire, the cart works in the office or at home, for the student or for anyone anywhere who needs to keep a number of papers and files organized and accessible on a regular basis. When not in use, the cart can be rolled to any storage area (a closet, a corner, or a spot under a table). Check your local variety, building, department, or closet stores for these.

FOR ADDITIONAL HELP

Stephanie Culp designs and implements systems and establishes procedures to help businesses and people get, and stay, organized. If you, your group, or company would like to have Stephanie help you get organized or serve as a speaker or trainer, you may contact her directly at:

Stephanie Culp
The Organization
Box 996
Montrose CA 91021
(818)248-0047

INDEX